THE BRONSON I KNEW

To my beloved wife, Boop, whose love and devotion have meant so much to me over our 52 years of marriage. It was Boop who, as a very special person with great understanding, shared me with so many nursing classes and came to know that she was the only one I loved.

Thank you, Boop, for your love and patience with me through the years.

THE BRONSON I KNEW

GONE BUT NOT FORGOTTEN

by

Dick Vander Molen

Alumni Association of
Bronson Methodist Hospital School of Nursing
2005

© 2005
Alumni Association of
Bronson Methodist Hospital School of Nursing

No part of this publication can be adapted, reproduced, stored in a retrieval system or transmitted in any form or by any means, electronic, mechanical, photocopying, recording, or otherwise without permission from the publisher.

ISBN 0-9763413-2-8

Vander Molen, Richard, 1929–
    The Bronson I knew, gone but not forgotten, by Dick Vander Molen. Kalamazoo, Mich.: Alumni Association of Bronson Methodist Hospital School of Nursing, 2005.
    xiv, 275 p. Includes photographs and index.

    1. Bronson Methodist Hospital (Kalamazoo, Mich.)—Staff 2. Hospitals—Michigan—Kalamazoo. I. Title
RA972.V238   362.V238

Printed by Fidlar Doubleday Inc., Kalamazoo, MI

TABLE OF CONTENTS

Foreword ix
Preface xi
1   The Journey Begins 1
2   Buffer Boy Richard 13
3   Young and Single in a Nurses' Dorm 39
4   Becoming An Electrician During Hospital Expansion in the Late 1940s 55
5   Early Photo History 86
6   A New Hospital and a New Life 91
7   Both the Hospital and My Family Grow in the 1950s 111
8   The Middle Years in Pictures 149
9   Death Takes Trusted Leaders and Good Friends 153
10   People, Expansion, Promotion 175
11   Late Photo History 191
12   Significant Events of the 1970s 197
13   Early 1980s — Retirement Ahead 211
14   Retirement Begins 219
Index 243

The Bronson I Knew

FOREWORD

Bronson Methodist Hospital School of Nursing and Dick Vander Molen fit together like a hand in glove. Over the years of Dick's employment at Bronson, he inspired scores of student nurses. The Alumni Association of Bronson Methodist Hospital School of Nursing (AABMHSN) had such respect and admiration for Dick that it awarded him an honorary diploma when he retired from the hospital.

Not only was Dick an inspiration to the student nurses, he was also their confidant, friend, listener, and sometimes a co-conspirator when a student nurse wanted to pull a "fast one" on a colleague. He touched students' lives in one way or another during their three years of residence in the dormitory. Everyone who knew Dick grew to love and appreciate him. He was always there for the students in times of need.

On May 10, 1952, Dick married Betty Gosling, a graduate of Bronson's class of 1951. She, too, was an inspiration and support for students. Her heart and home were open, providing a place of refuge and peace away from the constant stress of nursing classes and

The Bronson I Knew

clinical practice. Dick and Betty partnered as student caregivers, and continue their Bronson volunteer roles since their retirements and closure of the school.

The Alumni Association considers Dick's story as an important part of its history and that of the School of Nursing. His story is also an important piece of the history of the hospital. No one else has had the many years of experience and, therefore, gained as much insight into the minds of the Bronson's administrators who shaped the hospital's vision and values.

We're certain Dick's story will be read with interest, not only by graduates of Bronson Methodist Hospital School of Nursing, but by all who were touched by Dick and his caring, compassionate ways.

~

Board of Directors
Alumni Association of BMH School of Nursing

PREFACE

During my high school years, when I was working at Bronson Methodist Hospital, I would spend my study hours writing about my experiences at the nurses' dorm. I filed those notes away, along with notes about other experiences I had during my early years as the hospital electrician. Always in the back of my mind I thought it would be fun and interesting someday to share these events with fellow employees and especially the student nurses. I kept telling myself I would accomplish this seemingly insurmountable task "sometime."

Many graduate nurses, retirees and employees over the years, have said to me, "Dick, you need to write a book about your experiences at Bronson." When volunteering every Wednesday at the hospital, Bonnie Alkema kept telling me, "you need to start writing your book." However, without the encouragement of Anna Stryd, R.N., I probably would still be thinking of the day I would write about my life and my years at BMH. It was Anna who finally pushed me over the edge when she said, "Dick, you start writing and I will put it in the computer for you." So the journey began as I wrote in longhand and gave it to Anna, about 30 pages at a time. She returned it to me on typewritten pages, and so we did this for many months. It was her husband, Jack Stryd, who would look over the many typewritten pages and make suggestions, improvements, which was greatly appreciated. Thank you, Jack.

Anna and I met frequently, sometimes by phone, over lunch with Boop and Jack, or over a dish of ice cream at Lil' Ike's. We made corrections, suggestions and finally felt we had accomplished what I had set out to do. We were ready to go to print. A very special thanks, Anna, for the hours you put into this project.

My thanks also go to Hope College for granting me permission to reprint "The Slide." I would also like to thank my editor, Diane Worden, for her suggestions, words of advice and facilitating publication of my story. Without the support of the Alumni Association of Bronson Methodist Hospital School of Nursing, publication would have been much more difficult, and I will always be appreciative of the group's actions in support of this effort.

This book recounts many of my experiences at Bronson Methodist Hospital and the people I was fortunate to be associated with. Basically I relied on my memory of those early years. However, I have saved almost everything pertaining to Bronson and, in compiling my stories, I reviewed many of the notes, articles, publications and memos that I accumulated over the years. I also placed many phone calls to Bronson

Preface

alumni, retirees and Bill Brush. All of them proved to be invaluable sources of information.

My job as the hospital electrician allowed me access to all areas of the hospital and to all personnel. I came in contact with many interesting employees, some of whom I chose to share with readers. During my 60 years at Bronson Methodist Hospital, I was directly involved in the growth of the hospital and its continual state of remodeling. This was especially true during my years as Plant Maintenance manager. I really feel it's a story that only I can tell, and that's why I want to share it with all of you.

To support the Alumni Association of Bronson Methodist Hospital School of Nursing, all proceeds from this publication of my story will go to its scholarship fund.

~

Dick VanderMolen

The Bronson I Knew

1
THE JOURNEY BEGINS

My parents owned a farm in Decatur, Michigan. In the summer of 1920 they moved to Kalamazoo. They moved to a large house on Vine Street, across from Daleiden's Auto Body Shop. My dad had taken a job at the Kalamazoo Ice and Fuel Company. Our house backed up to the Upjohn football field where Kalamazoo Central played their home football games. The Balkema family lived next door to us, and they also had ten children. My family always talked about the good times we had with the Balkemas. The area occupied by these homes is now part of Upjohn Park.

On July 17, 1929 the world changed. Richard Vander Molen was born. I was born at Bronson Methodist Hospital, the youngest of ten children.

My being born must have changed my parent's lives too, because shortly thereafter we moved to Carr Street into a white house with a large porch. Carr is located off Portage Street between Vine and Lake streets. It was on Carr Street during those Depression years where I raised chickens and played with my dog Jiggs. My family loved to play cards, namely hearts. They sat around our large dining room table almost every night after supper playing hearts, while I listened to "The Lone Ranger" on the radio. Two boys I played with were both named John. Besides playing Cowboys and Indians and later shooting the Germans and the Japs, we would try to walk the railroad tracks from Vine to Lake without falling off. If we fell, we started over again. When I was 10 or 11 years old, I would catch crickets and night crawlers and sit on the corner of Carr and Portage streets for several hours with very little demand for my prize catches.

My next adventure was to mow lawns. This proved to be more profitable than selling bait because I had three jobs that paid twenty-five cents a lawn. At age 13 I bought a paper route for $15.00 that became a job which lasted for about two years. Although I enjoyed the small amount of money, it was discouraging trying to collect money every Saturday morning from people who said, "Come back later," or who didn't answer the door.

Between the ages of 12 and 15, I found myself at the Upjohn playground during the summer months. Mr. Steeby, a teacher at Washington Junior High School, was in charge of the playground where every afternoon and most evenings we had a ball game. The Emaar twins and the Van Loo twins, along with Kit Moerman and Vic and Thelma Comstock formed a tough team to beat. As I look back, it was Mr. Steeby who made the playground a fun place to be during those hot summer days.

The Journey Begins

Winter months found most of the Upjohn playground gang ice skating at the Crosstown Parkway pond. It's hard to believe but, years ago, the Crosstown Parkway ponds used to freeze over and we would ice skate on them. The City of Kalamazoo used tractors with brushes to keep the ice cleared of snow. Once a tractor fell through the ice. I can still smell the wood burning in the small shelter where we changed into our ice skates. On Saturday mornings we usually played hockey, and I would come home with my share of bruises. Two of the good players were Junior Ramer and Henry Naninga. After the 1940s, Crosstown pond was never again used for ice skating.

Searching for a Job

As I began my high school years at Kalamazoo Central High, I noticed job postings on the bulletin board. One of the jobs listed was a job feeding and taking care of rabbits and guinea pigs at Bronson Methodist Hospital. I went to talk with Mr. O.K. Christian, a counselor at Central, and he sent me to Bronson to meet with Dr. Hazel Prentice. I soon learned from Dr. Prentice that the words, "clean their cages," were left off the job posting.

The hospital laboratory was located in the basement of the hospital that was built in 1940 and faced Lovell Street. It was a six-story building with a large auditorium on the top floor. Dr. Prentice was a small woman whose office was located in a hallway off the main lab. Her office barely held a wooden desk and chair. Twice, while asking me my name, she was called to the main lab. On her return she said, "Let me show you what you are to do." We went up a stairwell in the back of the lab that led outdoors to a large stone and brick building called the Guild House, where dedicated women met during and after the war to sew bandages, etc.

The lab animals were kept in the basement of the Guild House. It was a dark and cold basement, and at the end of the hall was a place they called the paint shop. The hospital had one painter, and that's really all they needed as he very seldom dipped his paintbrush in a can of paint.

Dr. Prentice, with a key in her hand, opened the dark, dingy, and smelly room. When the lights were turned on the guinea pigs started to squeal. There were cages for about 15 pigs and maybe 10 for rabbits. The smell was not too pleasant, and the cages were a mess. The good news, as Dr. Prentice explained when I came in, was that I was to feed and water the animals first. The bad news was I had to clean their cages. I could do all this for thirty-five cents an hour! "When would you like me to start?" I asked. Big mistake.

"Now," she said, "and you can clean the rabbit cages first, we like them to be as clean as possible." It seemed to me to be an impossible task, and from the looks of them, I couldn't help but wonder if they had been cleaned at all in the last month. I was not to touch the pigs or rabbits—only clean their cages.

"How am I to clean their cages if I can't move them out?" I asked.

"No problem," Dr. Prentice said, "just clean the empty cages. I noticed the cages were filled with animal droppings. "We will move the rabbits before you get here."

"Did I ask you how old you are?" she asked.

"I'm 15 years old," I replied.

"In that case, you need a working permit, which you can get at the school administration building. When you get back, come to my office with your permit." It took less than three minutes to get to the administration office. The lady sitting behind the desk was Miss Adams, who had been my Sunday school teacher. She informed me that I could work 14 hours a week, and after several questions and signing papers, I returned to Dr. Prentice's office with my permit.

Dr. Prentice, who was the hospital pathologist and always busy, told me that I was to work two hours after school and four hours on Saturday. It was now after 4:30 P.M. and I thought I could go home and start the next day, but Dr. Prentice said. "You can get a good start on the rabbit cages tonight." Great Scot, I thought, how can I get out of this? I wasn't prepared to clean cages tonight or any night, I said to myself. How badly did I want to work for thirty-five cents an hour in a cold, dark, smelly basement? I said to Dr. Prentice, "How about if I just feed the animals tonight and clean cages tomorrow, because it's already past time for me to be home, and I know that my sister [whom I lived with] was probably wondering where I am."

"No problem," said Dr. Prentice, "just use my phone and call her."

The Rabbit Died on Friday

So I began my big adventure with the rabbits and pigs. As I recall, I didn't sign any papers or take a physical. Bronson didn't have Social Security yet. All they needed to know was my name and that I had a working permit. So I took the key and headed to the basement of the Guild House. As I opened the door, the pigs started squealing and I thought if the light ever goes out while I'm in here, the pigs are not the only ones who will be making a lot of noise.

I paced myself on that first night, taking my time feeding the animals knowing that I could work only two hours, leaving little time for cleaning cages. School, which never seemed to go fast, now sped by. I knew that those dirty cages had to be cleaned and they were waiting—just for me. The walk from Central to the Bronson lab took longer each day, as did the bike ride from Carr Street to Bronson Methodist Hospital on Saturdays.

The people in the lab were all friendly to me; maybe they were afraid that if I quit they would be cleaning cages again. Miss Elmore, second in command in the lab, always told me to do a good job on the cages, so I tried to avoid her, although I did get used to the job. Payday was every Friday, given to me in cash by Dr. Prentice. I became a little worried that I might get fired because on a few occasions when I came in after school a pig or rabbit looked to be dead and sure enough they were. How could this happen to me? I thought. They were OK when I left them. Maybe I gave them too much food or hadn't cleaned their cages the night before and their droppings got the better of them, as they often did to me.

Better tell Dr. Prentice, I thought. So off to her office I went, not knowing if I would lose my job. Fearful of what she would say, I started to apologize for the dead animals and I'll never forget her laughter as she said, "Don't worry, it's not your fault, as I did a little surgery on them. Just leave them alone and I'll take care of them later." Why would she want to do surgery on those animals? I wondered (as a 15-year old kid), and why did she laugh so loud? For the moment, I put it out of my mind and returned to my favorite pastime, singing to the live and dead animals as I cleaned their cages. I often sang or talked to the pigs and rabbits because it helped pass the time.

Forrest, the painter, would occasionally wander over from his paint shop. I guess it helped him pass the time of day to come and see my dead animals and me. I looked forward to Friday paydays. Dr. Prentice always came to see me at the Guild House basement with a brown envelope with four dollars and ninety cents in it. She would look around and say, "Dick, I think this cage needs to be cleaned." Little did she know that it was probably one I had just done.

Miss Anderson Intervenes

After two months with the last of many pigs, rabbits, and dirty cages, my time working for Dr. Prentice would soon come to an end. One night as I was leaving the hospital by the back entrance, which by the way was the emergency entrance, a tall nurse with high stiff-collared uniform stopped me and said, "Are you the boy who is working for Dr. Prentice?"

I answered, "Yes I am."

She asked, "Do you like your job cleaning rabbit cages?" Not knowing who she was or why she was asking me, I hesitated to answer.

Not telling her the truth that I really hated my job, I said, "I guess it's OK." She could tell by my answer that I wasn't too happy about my job.

She finally said, "I'm Miss Anderson, Director of Nurses, and I'm looking for a young boy to work in the nurses' dorm doing janitor work. Would you like to work for me?"

The Journey Begins

Would I? That was music to my ears. No more rabbits or guinea pig cages to clean, I thought. "When can I start?" I hoped tomorrow.

First, she said, "Tell Dr. Prentice that you are going to work for me and hopefully you can start right away." On the way home I thought about working in a nurses' dorm. What would it be like and what did I know about janitor duties? Better than cleaning cages!

Next was telling Dr. Prentice. It sort of scared me to think about it. All day in school I kept wondering what I would say to her. The walk from school to Bronson took longer than usual as I kept saying over and over again, "Dr. Prentice, thank you for allowing me to work for you and taking care of the animals, but yesterday a Miss Anderson asked me to work for her in the nurses' dorm and I really want to." Guess what? Dr. Prentice wasn't in and wouldn't be in for two days! It was the longest two days of my young life. I didn't know where to find Miss Anderson so I couldn't tell her Dr. Prentice wasn't in. Finally, D-Day arrived and I asked Dr. Prentice if I could see her. She laughed and said, "More dead rabbits?"

"No, nothing like that. A Miss Anderson wants me to work for her," I finally blurted out. Now I really had her attention for the first time in two months.

"I have no one to take your place," she said, "and besides, I need you." Wow, I must have been doing a better job than I thought—no it couldn't be that—it's instead a job that no one wants. "Well," she finally said, "you can't leave me until you find someone to take your place."

Whitewashing Aunt Polly's Fence

Now my work was cut out for me, a super salesman I would have to be. Who could I tap for this lousy job? It couldn't be a friend—I wouldn't wish that job on anyone. Yet, if I didn't find someone soon, I might lose my job in the nurses' dorm. My neighborhood playmate, John—would I dare ask him? Nothing to lose so I said, "John there's a great job at Bronson that I thought you might like—it's working in the Bronson lab with animals. It pays thirty-five cents an hour and you can work after school and on Saturdays. I'll help you get a working permit, and if after a few weeks you don't like it, you can quit."

Working with animals sounded like fun to John. Little did he know, I thought. So John and I went to see Dr. Prentice, and she asked me to show him his job. I could tell he wasn't too impressed. I should note that the night before I showed him around, I did an extra good job making the cages clean, so the smell was not like I experienced two months earlier. Convincing him wasn't that hard. John took the job and I was free to work in the nurses' dorm. Now to find Miss Anderson.

I was told that her office was on the first floor behind the hall near the cashier's desk. There were three offices at the end of the hall—one straight ahead, one to the right and one to the left. A man sitting in the first office said, "I am Mr. Gibson, are you looking for someone?" After telling him I was looking for a Miss Anderson, he asked, "Is it important? She is in a meeting." To me it was very important, so that was what I told him.

He made a phone call and in a few minutes Miss Anderson came out and said, "Are you ready to work for me and is it OK with Dr. Prentice?" I said it was OK because I had found another boy to take my place.

And so, my days with the pigs and rabbits come to an end, and I was ready to grow into a new and more exciting job.

~

P.S. I never knew they were used for pregnancy testing.

The Bronson I Knew

2

BUFFER BOY RICHARD

Mrs. Kirk and the Dorm

"Let's get going and get you started." So Miss Anderson and I walked through a patient area she called Hall 1 to the nurse's dorm, where she introduced me to a lady who was the housemother. "Mrs. Kirk, this is the boy I promised you." Mrs. Kirk was a soft-spoken lady who asked me my name. I said it was Dick. She told me she had a son named Richard and that was what she wanted to call me. Miss Anderson told Mrs. Kirk to show me what I was to do, and left, not even knowing what my last name was.

We first walked to the elevator and she said:

> See this button? It's what we call the "man bell button," and you are to ring the bell on the second and third floor when you go to one of those floors so the girls will know you are coming on their floor. Be sure when you ring it twice, you go to the second floor—not the third floor. When you leave the second floor, come back to the first

floor and ring the bell three times before going up there.

That was easy, but why did she put so much emphasis on it? Only a short time later did I realize the importance of letting the girls know which floor I was on.

The closet near the front door held a floor buffer and a big dust mop that I was to use every night after school and on Saturday morning. The big brass rails on the stairwells had to be kept shiny with a special polish. The iceboxes on the second and third floor (no refrigerators) had to have ice in them, and I was to supply them with milk, bread and peanut butter from the hospital's main kitchen. My job was to do this in addition to supplying North and South homes with the same items—wherever *they* were. I would soon find out.

These were my duties, along with others she would tell me about later. I could tell I was going to like Mrs. Kirk, even if she wanted to call me Richard. She was a kind lady and, as the days and months passed by, I knew she thought of me as her son.

Learning to Run the Buffer

Nurses were everywhere. Do I dare speak to them as I run the dust mop past the Coke machine, library and nursing office? Most looked to be in their twenties and only a few said "Hi." I was anxious to get a look at the second and third floors, to ring the man bell for the first time, and to ride the elevator. As luck would have it, Mrs.

Kirk said, "Richard, you need to buff this floor that you just dust mopped." Learning to run the buffer was easier than I thought and, as time went by, it became "my buffer." After all, I soon would be known as, "Dick the Buffer Boy." Ringing the man bell and riding the elevators with my buffer to the second floor with Mrs. Kirk, was an experience. The elevator never leveled with the floor; there was a button on the elevator that allowed you to level the elevator to floor level. After several times of going too high and then too low, I finally got it leveled and we got off.

Instructions from Mrs. Kirk

For the first time I saw the rooms where the nurses lived. I plugged my buffer cord in a janitor closet at the end of the hall as Mrs. Kirk gave me my instructions and stood by.

> You may dust mop the hall and then buff it. We have a maid to dust mop the girls' room and if they ask you, you may buff their rooms. There is also a kitchen on each floor that you are to buff as well. The large room at the end of this hall is the apartment of Miss Sweet, the Nursing Arts Instructor. You need not buff her floor unless she asks you to.

I noticed a large bathroom and a small kitchen. Most of the rooms on the second floor seemed small. At the end of the hall, past the elevator, was a door that Mrs.

Kirk said was a medical floor of the hospital called "2 West."

Riding to the third floor, several nurses rode with us and Mrs. Kirk told them—"This is our new boy, Richard. I want you to be nice to him." I felt a little embarrassed and wondered what these nurses thought of this little freckled-faced 15-year-old kid. The rooms on the third floor were much larger than the ones on the second floor. There was also a door into the hospital, which Mrs. Kirk said I was never to go through—the OB floor.

After finishing up on the third floor, Mrs. Kirk said, "Richard, put your buffer away, and come to my office." Her apartment was next to the big lounge on the first floor. She wanted me to tell her about my family and myself. When I told her my mother died when I was 11 years old, I could feel her compassion and she never treated me as my boss—only as her little boy.

Finding the Cafeteria and Herman

I began my second day at the big dorm, as it was called by the nurses, and Mrs. Kirk told me that I was to go the kitchen located in the basement past the cafeteria and ask for a man named Herman. He would show me where to get a cart to bring ice, milk, bread and peanut butter for the kitchens on the second and third floors, and to the kitchens at North and South homes.

At this point I didn't know where the kitchen was or where to find North and South homes. Taking the steps to the basement, I noticed the hospital laundry in the corner of the basement and I knew not to go that way. Turning right at the bottom of the steps, I followed the hall to the cafeteria. It was a large room. I went inside, looking for Herman, with my requisition slip. "Herman, where are you?" I kept saying to myself. Finally after asking a few women where I could find Herman, I was able to locate him. He was a short man and a little on the stout side. I told him my name and that I was a new kid on the block and working for Mrs. Kirk.

"Well, kid," he said, "this is the cart you are to use, here is where we keep the ice, and if there is none in here, you will have to pull it up yourself from here—we make our own ice in 100# metal containers. I will show you how to do it. I'll also show you where to get the bread and peanut butter. If I'm not here, give your slip to one of the women."

So, with the ice and food on the cart, I headed back to the dorm and the man bell. After putting the ice and food away, I asked for directions to North and South homes. North Home was on the corner of Lovell and John streets. The kitchen was in the back of the house, which I found out after going to the front door and meeting a friendly lady named Mrs. Conklin. Leaving North Home, I crossed John Street to South Home, which was across from the big dorm. This time I went to the back door and up the steps to the kitchen. I didn't see anyone so I yelled, "Is anyone home?" A lady came, who said she was Miss Coleman, the housemother, and she told me where to put the ice and food. After two days on the job, I had seen where the nurses called "home away from home."

Anything Else You Need Done?

Heading back to the hospital, I just knew that this was going to be a fun job, nothing like those rabbits and pigs. After school at 3:30 P.M., I sometimes found myself running part way to Bronson. Spring was in the air and also in my feet, as I made my way through the front door of the big dorm. I was always to check with Mrs. Kirk first to see if there was something that needed to be done before I started to buff the floors. Today she told me that a Miss Moffat, who was a registered nurse and the advisor to the freshman class, needed to have some boxes moved from her room on the third floor of the dorm to the sixth floor auditorium. Following Miss Moffat to the sixth floor was my first adventure past the kitchen. I was impressed with the large auditorium and the nurses who rode on the elevator with us.

My Introduction to Floyd and Others

On our way back to the dorm, we met a man with a dark blue suit and bow tie. He wore large horn-rimmed glasses. Miss Moffat introduced me to Floyd Rothwell, chief engineer at the hospital. He shook my hand and said, "Come to my office sometime and I'll show you the boiler room."

"Thanks, I will" I said, not knowing where his office was.

This was a great place to work I thought, everyone was so friendly. After several weeks I got to know some of the girls by name. I also met Miss Sweet, who I thought was Florence Nightingale. The freshmen on the third floor were always kidding with me, especially Wanda Grauman and Jane Mayfield. Many times after supplying the kitchens with food, the girls invited me to join them in their gab sessions. It was an education different than the one I was getting at Kalamazoo Central. I was now meeting new people:

- George, the mailman, who was popular with the girls, bringing mail and packages from home
- Mrs. Haines in the nursing office
- Miss Roe, the head housekeeper, whom I received my janitor supplies from
- Harvey Meyers, laundry manager, where I took the dirty uniforms and brought back the clean, starched ones
- Herman Heystek, the man in charge of the X-ray Department, who stopped in one day and said, "Are you a Vander Molen?"

"Yes," I said.

"Well, I've seen you at the church YMCA baseball games where I've played against your brothers and the First Reformed team."

- The Coca-Cola man, Jim, who I looked forward to seeing each week so I could fill the coke machine and drink a few while I was doing it.

Calling Cards

Two small libraries were directly across from the coke machine, where girls were trying to study. If I made too much noise filling the machine, they kindly let me know, by saying, "Richard, *be quiet*, we have a test we are studying for." Must be that they heard Mrs. Kirk call me Richard.

On several occasions, while working on the second and third floors, the girls forgot I was on the floor and would leave their room with only their slip or less on, to go to the bathroom or kitchen. They would say, "Dick, I didn't know you were here," or "Why didn't you ring the man bell?" Most of the time I didn't get a chance to say I did ring it, because of their quick exit.

There were times while working on the third floor, I was unable to call the elevator because it was out of order; so I would walk down the steps and to let the girls know I was coming, I would yell, "Man overboard." Several times the notice came too late, as I would catch someone half-dressed. "Man overboard," was my calling card when I would go on the floors, even if I rang the man bell.

One day I noticed several nurses wearing a different uniform and I asked Mrs. Kirk why they were not wearing white uniforms. She told me they were Cadet nurses. I was impressed. Working in the dorm, I had to punch a time card, which I hadn't had to do in the laboratory. As I could only work for two hours, I would punch out, and continue to work or at least hang around and talk with the girls.

Summer Job

It was now the month of June and school would soon be out. Wondering if I could work more hours during the summer months, I went back to the school administration building to see Miss Adams. I was still only 15 years old and wouldn't be 16 until July 17. I was given a permit to work 30 hours a week. That was music to my ears! Bronson was now my second home and I loved my job. Summer time meant many changes—seniors were talking about graduation and freshmen were going on vacation. They would be moving to South Home on their return, with the junior class occupying North Home. I didn't get acquainted with too many seniors as several were on affiliations. They were the class of '45, 38 nurses in all and soon to graduate. Elaine Hecht, in the senior class, always stopped to talk to me, along with Marge Edgerton.

Riding my bike to work usually took about 10 minutes. I always parked it outside the back entrance of the dorm and never had to lock it. Sometimes the girls would take it for a ride. The back of the hospital had a horseshoe driveway off Cedar Street. Ambulances, with their sirens blasting away, would come bringing patients to the emergency room. Usually it was G. Ray Hall, a short, little man, driving the ambulance. Inside this horseshoe area, there was room for maybe 15 cars to park, mostly for doctors. Also there was a small garden area where the women in the hot laundry could take a break. I would, on occasion, join them, while yelling to the girls in the dorm. The back of the dorm entrance could be used for girls to sneak in at night from a date, or so I was told. I was now working five hours a day, six days a week, 8:00 A.M.–1:30 P.M. with one-half hour for lunch.

I knew it was wrong . . . Eating in the cafeteria was always a great place for hearing the latest grapevine news. The cafeteria consisted of one large room for nurses and two small dining rooms—one for doctors and administration and the other for maintenance, housekeeping, laundry and kitchen help. Meals, which were fifty cents, included the main meal, salad, dessert and beverage. Grace, who was the cashier, sat just inside the cafeteria door and would on several occasions give me my money back. She would always smile and say, "Thank you, Dick." What a kind lady to save me fifty cents, I thought, but I admit I knew it was wrong. Tillie, a white-haired lady, was the supervisor in the kitchen. I liked Tillie. She was a Tiger fan, and we would talk about Hank Greenberg and the rest of the Detroit Tigers.

On the way to the cafeteria from the dorm was the hospital morgue, where one day I saw Dr. Prentice for the first time since I started working in the dorm. Her first words to me were, "That boy you got to work in your place quit." No surprise to me and I didn't ask her who was taking care of the pigs and rabbits now.

From Buffing to Mopping

It's now summer, and I soon learn that my work load increased to mopping and waxing the girls rooms, after moving beds and dressers in the hall. It wasn't as bad as it sounds because it gave me a chance to visit with the girls while waiting for the floors to dry. There was a room on the third floor overlooking John Street. Outside of this room there was a porch roof where the girls could go out and sunbathe. The other favorite spot to sunbathe was the roof off the sixth floor auditorium. "This job looks better all the time," I said to myself as I saw the girls in their bathing suits.

In the summer of 1945, the maple twin beds, desks and dressers in all the rooms on the second floor were replaced with bunk beds, blond dressers and desks, the same as on third floor. Mary B. Anderson took charge of telling everyone what went where and how it was to be done. It was the first time I saw her authority, but not the last.

While she was there she said she had a small job for me to do over at the staff home on Cedar Street, which was next door to the hospital. I was to come over on Saturday at 10:00 A.M. I told Mrs. Kirk I had to see Miss Anderson about a small job, which turned out to be washing and waxing her black Oldsmobile. Some small job—it took the rest of my working day to finish, but I said to myself if it wasn't for Mary B. (as many called her), I could still be with the pigs and rabbits.

Refrigerators—Less Ice to Deliver

In July refrigerators replaced iceboxes on the second and third floors of the dorm. A year later they were replaced at North and South homes. So my ice load began to decrease in late summer. Mrs. Richardson and Mrs. Rinehart were two of the maids that worked in the dorm. Both looked to be in their late 60s, or so it seemed to me. They worked basically on the first floor sorting uniforms, cleaning Mrs. Kirk's apartment, the nursing office, etc. The second and third floors each had one maid who always gave me some motherly advice, whether I wanted it or not, but later came to appreciate.

World War II was over in Germany, but much of the talk was about when it would be over in Japan. On several occasions I would see a soldier or sailor coming to the dorm to see his girlfriend.

Fruit Cellar

Bronson had a fruit cellar located in a room in the basement across from the elevator. It actually ran under the grassy area near the dorm entrance. The Methodist women supplied the hospital with canned jars of pears, peaches, plums, tomatoes, and beans. Many times I would help Herman stack the jars in the damp fruit cellar. He was always grateful for my help and now called me Dick, instead of kid. These jars of fruit were not only used for patients, but also served in the cafeteria. It was tasty, and also helped save the hospital money.

Getting ready for new students . . . Toward the end of August the big dorm was empty. My job now was to mop and wax all the rooms, getting ready for the freshman class of 1948. My only contact with the girls came when they would come to the dorm to get their mail or uniforms, or to check with Mrs. Haines in the nursing office. I could also see them at North and South homes, and standing in line at the cafeteria.

Floyd and I Meet Again

The small dining room was the place where I met Floyd Rothwell again, along with Roy VandenBerg, the hospital carpenter; Jack Tribe, the window and wall washer; Glenn Stanley, the electrician; and my friend Forrest Potter, the painter from my pig and rabbit days. One day after lunch, Floyd said, "Would you like to see the boiler room, if you have the time?" Mrs. Kirk never kept close track of me, so time was something I never worried about.

To get to the boiler room you took the stairway near the X-ray Department past Mrs. Roe's small office, going down the steps and reaching Floyd's office, which consisted of a desk and a long wooden bench. You then went down a flight of steel steps where the two hospital boilers were. I met a Mr. Bill Wiggins, the fireman, who was sweating from shoveling coal into the boilers. After

The Bronson I Knew

making a tour of the boiler room, I thanked Floyd and made my way back to the dorm to continue waxing the rooms and halls.

During the long hot summer, there were only a few girls in the dorm and only the maids to talk with. Mrs. Kirk always thought I was working too hard and insisted I come to her office and rest. I think she was lonely and just wanted to talk to me.

We Learn the Bomb Was Dropped

I remember the day in August when the first atom bomb was dropped on Japan. I was eating in the small dining room with some of the maintenance men. Later Glenn said, "Dick, have you ever been on the sixth floor roof?" Of course I hadn't, so we took the elevator to the sixth floor, went through the auditorium to the roof and looked over the city. Glenn wanted to talk about the atom bomb and told me we didn't know what awesome power has been released on mankind. I'll never forget his concern and the impact it had on me. We must have stayed up there for an hour talking about it.

The War Ends, A New Era Begins

It's now August. On the day World War II ended, I rode my bike to Upjohn Park to see my friends, but the park was empty. It was a funny feeling not to see anyone. I returned home and heard on the radio that downtown Kalamazoo was celebrating, so I rode my bike to the hospital, parked it in back of the dorm and joined the crowd on Burdick Street. Later I sat on the front porch of

North Home with several of the girls, yelling as cars drove by. They were all honking their horns. It was truly a night to celebrate and remember.

The next day at the hospital everyone was happy and Dr. Perdew, the hospital superintendent whom I hadn't yet met, asked those who could, to come to the sixth floor auditorium for prayer and thanksgiving. Dr. Perdew talked and prayed, and then we all read aloud a printed prayer:

Prayer for Peace
Almighty and Eternal God, who dost hold the destiny of nations in the hollow of Thy hand, we acknowledge, with a gratitude too deep for words, that divine mercy which has sustained us through the dark and bitter years of war, and that divine power which had brought us to the day of victory. Before Thee we cherish the precious memory of those who have spilled their lifeblood in the defense of America. Receive them unto Thyself, we pray; and may They Spirit overshadow, with the divine comfort, the hearts which are lonely for the touch of a vanished hand and the sound of a voice that is still. . . .

Grant, O Lord, that brutal aggression may never again be permitted to loose its fury upon mankind. Enable us as a notion to assume our full share in the building of a peace so just and so enduring as to be worthy of the costly sacrifice which this conflict has exacted.

> *And now, may Thy healing Presence bind up the wounds of our war torn humanity and teach all nations to walk together in justice and good will, through the grace of Jesus Christ, Our Lord, Amen.*

Many had tears in their eyes as we left the auditorium. With the end of the war, the class of '45 was all excited about their boyfriends coming home, diamonds and getting married.

It's September and there was talk of graduation at the First Methodist Church. Nurses I haven't seen before have just returned from Children's Hospital in Detroit and from Mayberry. Mrs. Kirk informed me that a new class would be arriving soon. It all sounded exciting. New girls to meet—but will I ever see the seniors again that I fell in love with this past summer?

I attended my first graduation at the First Methodist Church—28 nurses in all received their pins and diplomas. It was always an exciting and happy time, but also sad in a way, because I knew that there were many that I would never see again.

The Class of 1948 Enters Training

September 16th was fast approaching. The dorm sparkled with all floors waxed, brass railing shining, and beds made; waiting for the freshmen class of '48, I am now back at school and since I have turned 16 years old, I can work 24 hours a week. Mary B. Anderson gave me a ten-cent raise so now I'm making forty-five cents an hour. Mrs. Kirk asked me if I would be willing to help with the luggage when the new class arrived. What better way for me to meet the new girls than to help them carry in their luggage and show them to their rooms—and I guess it wouldn't hurt if I mentioned that I was "Dick the Buffer." The luggage sure was heavy, but I didn't mind, after all I had 38 girls to get acquainted with. Helping move the luggage, which I volunteered to do for the next several years, was a job I always enjoyed.

I remember well my first day with the class of '48. It was after school and as I rang the man bell and went to buff and dust mop the halls; I saw the surprise of many girls, wondering what a boy was doing in the dorm. Did Mrs. Kirk forget to tell them about me or the man bell, I wondered. Doors to their rooms that were once opened now closed as I ran my large dust mop down the hall. Things seemed so different. The other girls, now living in North and South homes were so friendly to me. Later I made my way to North and South homes with the ice and food supplies, and it seemed so good to be greeted with friendly smiles. The next few days were not much better as only a few girls spoke to me. I was so excited about a new class of girls coming to the dorm, but now I was not too sure. Finally one of the girls on the second floor said hi to me while I was running my buffer and asked me my name.

"Dick," I said, and she said, "my name is Bertha Spitters." Shortly after that many girls started to speak and tell me their names.

On the third floor was the stairwell to the large wooden attic, where girls could store their suitcases from home. It didn't take long for the girls to ask me to carry them up for them. When they found out I supplied their kitchens with food, everyone suddenly knew my name. One of the girls, Connie Claflin, asked if I could find something that they could put their many books into. After looking around I finally came up with a wooden orange crate from the kitchen. After the girls decorated it with a skirt, it looked great and held many books. The demand for more orange crates increased and continued through many successive classes.

The Cranky Dorm Elevator

The dorm elevator was always an adventure to ride, as it was only able to hold ten people and, as I said earlier, never leveled at floor level. One day while riding down from the third floor with several girls, the elevator stopped between floors for no apparent reason. The only thing we could do was to ring the bell inside the elevator. As far as I could tell, the only people that were concerned were Mrs. Kirk and Mrs. Haines. After a half an hour, Floyd Rothwell showed up and said he would get us out in a few minutes—not to panic. I don't remember that we did, right Reva Banker? It was something that we all talked about later. Girls were now starting to take pictures and Ginny McPhail took one of me running my buffer, that in later years appeared in the yearbook.

The class of '48 was now getting used to me yelling, "Man overboard" so they knew I was there. No smoking was allowed in the big dorm, but some of the seniors went to Miss Anderson, herself a heavy smoker, and got approval for a smoking room on the first floor next to the two rooms called the infirmary rooms. Mrs. Kirk didn't think that was a good location, especially with sick girls in the next rooms.

One day Mrs. Kirk said, "Richard, I want you to paint this small iron table red. I'll give you some money and you go over to Sherwin–Williams paint store on Burdick Street to get a small can of red paint." When I got there a small older man, who looked to me to be in his 70s, waited on me.

When I got ready to pay him I innocently said to him, "Are you Mr. Williams or Mr. Sherwin?" He didn't think I was funny and got very upset. I wasn't trying to be funny—I thought he owned the store, not knowing it was a large national chain. When I told Mrs. Kirk, she had a good laugh.

A Hospital Patient Myself

One day after I finished buffing on the third floor, I was standing next to the telephone while winding up the buffer cord. There was only one telephone on each floor. I was talking to several girls when I noticed some loose tape on the buffer cord. I pulled out my pocketknife to cut off the tape. For some reason, maybe because I was talking to the girls, I decided to close the knife on my leg. Bad mistake, because the knife did not snap shut, but went straight into my right leg, cutting an artery. I pulled out the knife and the blood came pouring out.

Now there was real panic and the girls, being freshmen, didn't know what to do. Finally four or five girls decided to take me to ER. We ran to the dorm elevator, took it to the back dorm entrance, and walked to the emergency room. No one was there. We pushed a button that rang a bell in surgery where a nurse was assigned to ER. She had to run down four flights of stairs with the key to ER. With blood all over my pants and on the floor, we were all getting nervous, especially me, wondering if I had any blood left. I was really feeling faint and know the four or five freshmen were too, before the nurse finally arrived. On the ER table, pressure was applied to my leg to stop the bleeding. Dr. Howard Jackson just happened to be leaving the hospital, so the nurse called him in. Not ever having a doctor, I now had one. I was admitted to 2 West where I spent the next six days.

My first visitor was Mary B. Anderson, who wanted to know exactly how I got hurt. Back then we didn't have accident forms to fill out, so she wanted to know in detail what happened. Mrs. Miller was in charge of 2 West and when so many student nurses came to see me, she posted a "no visitor" sign. My room was next to the dorm, so after the 7:00–3:30 P.M. shift went home, the girls came over to see me. Dr. Howard Jackson, with his bow tie, came to see me everyday and ordered penicillin shots, which I didn't care about. The R.N. who took care of me most of the time was Mrs. Maxwell, a sweet and kind lady.

I missed several days of school, which I made up later. I returned to work in a week, with no more knives in my pockets. I never got a bill from the hospital or from Dr. Jackson. It was the first of many times that I was to be a patient in the hospital.

Getting Used to Doctors

Across the street from the big dorm was the office building of Drs. Boys, Jennings and Gerstner. These doctors would always use the front entrance of the big dorm and go through 1 West to the hospital. Drs. Boys and Gerstner were the kind and fatherly type and always spoke to me. I was really afraid of Dr. Jennings, he usually only managed a gruff, "Hi."

When I was waxing the first floor hall floors, I would lock the front door and post a sign, "Door Locked for Waxing, Please Use Back Door." That would upset Dr. Jennings. One day when I locked the door for waxing, Helen Morgan, a freshman student, came back from downtown and found the door locked and had to go around to the back door. When she came in through the back entrance, I overheard her say to one of the girls, "That brat kid had me locked out." Now that really hurt and you can tell I never forgot it!

Helping Out

The sign-out book was located across from the elevator on the first floor. I always checked on certain girls who I might have had a crush on, to see where they were going and when they would be coming back. On several occasions a girl would ask me to sign her in after she was gone for several hours. I never questioned them why. I just made sure I wasn't seen doing it. Luckily I never got caught, nor did they.

The freshman class always had a special bus to take them to Western for classes, but they had to walk back after class. I especially remember how cold some looked in the winter months, so I always made sure the front door was never locked. I remember when the class of '48 was going home for Thanksgiving, many for the first time since coming into training. I talked to some of them later and said they almost decided not to come back to training.

Wait 'til I'm seventeen . . Well, where has time gone? It's almost Christmas and guess what? I know all the freshmen by name now, as well as the junior and seniors. Most of the talk was about the Christmas formal at Walwood Hall and the veterans from Western being invited. This was my first Christmas at Bronson and everyone was giving me candy and cookies. How could I stay so thin? There was mistletoe hanging over the sign-out book, but I guess nobody wanted to kiss a 16-year-old kid. But I tell myself, wait until next year when I will be 17.

It's been ten months now since I started working at Bronson and I'm really learning my way around the hospital and meeting many employees—Lyle Nottingham, Jack Tribe, Thelma Groat, Marion Smith, and Bill Van Haaften and a special friend Shirley Evans, to mention a few.

It was after school one day in February that the freshman class was all excited about capping to be held in the sixth floor auditorium, I believe. The next day a few were proud to show me their new caps, and I took several pictures for them.

Softball and Tennis

With spring in the air and on the playground behind Harding School on the corner of Lovell and Jasper streets, we managed several softball games. I was always the umpire, but I was never sure if the girls really knew the rules. Tennis was another favorite sport and was played at Upjohn Park, only a few blocks away. I played tennis with many of the girls and managed to win a game or two.

It's the end of May—the junior class at South Home still enjoyed parties, food and gab session, so whenever I was over there, they invited me to have goodies with them and asked me what was going on over at the big dorm. I told them everything I could remember.

Messenger Boy

At North Home on the corner of John and Lovell streets, I often managed time to sit on the large front porch with one or two girls—namely, Betty Brown or Veva Lou Whitehead. They wanted to know about the juniors at South Home. Sounds like I was a messenger boy, and for the most part I guess I was.

No freshmen here . . . I was soon to learn about Hell Week, not from Mrs. Kirk, but from several seniors who told me that the freshmen students would be their slaves for one week. Several times during Hell Week, when the phone would ring on either second or third floors, the girls asked me to answer it and tell the senior who was calling that there were no freshmen on the floor. It wasn't long before I decided not to answer the phone when it rang—I didn't care to get involved or take sides. It was "hide and seek week" for the seniors and freshmen. Looking back, I did feel sorry for several of my favorite freshmen when they were slaves making beds, cleaning shoes, setting up uniforms and carrying trays, etc. It all ended when the seniors gave the freshmen class a party, to ease their conscience, I'm sure.

It's summer, and the freshman class will soon be going on vacation and leave the dorm for North Home. They keep telling me that when they come back they will have their junior bands for their caps.

Reflections of My First Year at Bronson

This first year has gone by fast for me, but I remembered so many things. To mention only a few:

- listening to the gab sessions in the small kitchens in the dorm and at North and South homes
- girls getting their diamonds
- talk of state boards
- patients and times at State Hospital
- girls not wanting to work on men's or women's wards
- seeing girls cry for any reason (always bothered me)
- not wanting to scrub with certain doctors
- hating to work in Central Supply or the Diet Kitchen

~

The Bronson I Knew

3
YOUNG AND SINGLE
IN A NURSES' DORM

Changes Come with the Class of '49

Summer meant a repeat performance for me, getting ready for a new class of student nurses. As I turned 17 years old on the 17th of July, I knew that it would be my last year as Dick the Buffer because I would be a senior at Kalamazoo Central High School. That summer Jack Tribe began washing walls at the big dorm, and I offered to help him. Jack had a small problem. He often left the hospital to skip over to the Home Restaurant for a beer or two and would say to me, "Dickie Boy," as he called me, "just keep working, and I'll be back shortly." Shortly, to Jack, was two or three hours, but I didn't mind covering for him.

Toward the end of the summer Mrs. Kirk informed me that 30 freshmen students would be arriving on September 16. That was the good news. With tears in her eyes, she told me the bad news—she was leaving for New Mexico to serve at an Indian reservation. She said, "Richard, I'm going to miss you, you have been my little boy. I will write to you, and you let me know what you're doing." I was crushed. Mrs. Kirk had been so good to me and now she was leaving. Neither one of us could say much, she gave me a hug and went into her apartment. I had forgotten to ask her when she would be leaving—it was only three days after she told me that she left. She did not want to say good-bye, but left a letter on my buffer for me. I lost a dear friend who was like a second mother to me. I must have moped around for a week, when Miss Anderson finally informed me that a Mrs. Wright would be arriving to take Mrs. Kirk's place. I wanted to tell her no one could take Mrs. Kirk's place, but I didn't.

I'm hard to keep track of? After meeting Mrs. Wright, I found she was not at all like Mrs. Kirk, who gave me the free run of the dorm. Mrs. Wright thought it necessary to keep track of me—I don't know why. It was just one of many other changes that summer:

- A new maid appeared on third floor named Ruby Smith, who came to be a good friend.
- Miss Melson replaced Mrs. Haines in the nursing office.
- Mrs. Howell replaced Miss Coleman at South Home.
- Mrs. Ellis was the new housemother at North Home, replacing Mrs. Conklin.

Well, despite Mrs. Wright, the dorm was ready for the probies of the class of '49. But before they arrived came good-byes to the class of 1946. Their graduation took place at the First Methodist Church, my second graduation ceremony for a nursing class.

September 16, and here we go again—carrying luggage for 30 girls. This class of girls looked younger and was friendlier than last year's class. By the way, I had helped last year's class move all their possessions with the help of the laundry cart and the old wooden morgue cart to North Home. My first meeting with Mrs. Ellis, the new housemother, proved her to be a friendly lady, a little on the heavy side. I could tell I was going to like her.

Need to know those names . . . The buzz around the hospital was the talk about expansion and the need for an additional 100 beds. The guys in the Maintenance Department were talking about it in the dining room. They don't think it will happen because of the money to be raised for such a major project. However, the hospital board made the decision to expand the hospital to 240 beds. As for me, I just sat and listened, as I had more important things to think about—like learning the names of 30 new girls. I decided it was easier for me to learn their names if I concentrated on the girls according to their room. I didn't do it that way the previous year and it took me quite awhile to remember all their names. By the end of October, I was excited to be able to call them all by name.

Love that class . . . Kalamazoo Central had a special class for both girls and boys. I can't recall what it was called, but it was how to interact with the opposite sex,

The Bronson I Knew

dating, relationships, about what we did after school, etc. When it came to my turn to say what I did after school, I said I worked at Bronson Methodist Hospital in the nurses' dorm and I was the only male allowed on the floors. Believe me—I had everyone's attention. They had all kinds of questions for me; even the teacher joined in. Every week after that I felt like the main person in the class. The class lasted only eight weeks, but suddenly I had a lot of new friends.

Dorm Experiences

Hiding from Mrs. Wright became a game for me. If I was on the third floor talking to the girls near the elevator and heard it coming up, I ran down one flight of stairs to the second floor yelling, "Man overboard," on my way to the first floor. I made it a point to be doing something on the first floor when she got back. I could tell by the look on her face that she wanted to ask where I had been. I'm sure she knew I wasn't on the first floor when she came looking for me. This was repeated many, many times during the two or three years Mrs. Wright was housemother.

I'll never be the same . . . Riding the dorm elevator was always an exciting experience. I mentioned earlier, several of us had been stuck between floors. But one experience I had was with a freshman student nurse. She was good-looking and always teasing me. On occasion she did it when Mrs. Wright was around, and I thought I was going to get in trouble. One day I got on the elevator with my buffer and on jumped my playful friend. She ran the elevator as we headed for the third floor. Suddenly she stopped the elevator between floors, turned off the lights and planted a long—and I mean LONG—kiss on me. I had mixed emotions, I sort of enjoyed the kiss, but I was worried about anyone finding out about it. I can honestly say that it was the only time I rode the elevator alone with her again. However, when she arranged to miss class at Western a few times and we were likely the only ones on the third floor, she managed to educate me on the art of kissing. I guess she missed too many classes so she or someone else decided her days as a student nurse were over, and so were my private lessons. Thankfully, my eight-week class at Kalamazoo Central was over, so I didn't share any of this with the class, although I'm sure they would have been excited to hear it.

The Annex . . . In between the dorm and North Home was a gray house called the Annex. It was used for a variety of things—a classroom, dorm for senior students, quarters for residents and finally a lab for electrocardiography.

The girls who lived at the Annex had it made. They had no housemother and were basically on their own, although they had to be in at certain hours, or so they were told. I always stopped at the Annex on my way to North Home to deliver bread, milk and peanut butter and, of course, visit the girls. Mrs. Wright always complained that I took too much time to re-supply the food. Of course I did, but I considered it one of the perks of my job, even if she didn't. I did spend time at North

The Bronson I Knew

and South homes visiting with Mrs. Ellis and Mrs. Howell.

Poor Mrs. Howell. She was a small, kind lady who thought I worked too hard and insisted that I come into her apartment where she told me to rest and take a nap, and she would be back to wake me up. I didn't want to hurt her feelings so I would sit for maybe 15 minutes and get back to work, thanking her for being so kind to me. The other thing she did was to try and fatten me up, giving me cookies and candy bars.

A penny for your thoughts . . . I mentioned earlier about all the jars full of fruit that were delivered to the hospital. Well, all the empty jars were stored in the basement of North Home. I took my share of them to stack on shelves and on the floor. It seemed to me that there must have been a thousand of them. A few years after the war ended, the fruit canned by the Methodist women came to an end. So, what to do with all of those jars? Bronson received an offer, I can't remember from whom, to give the hospital one cent for each jar. Dr. Perdew said he wanted two cents per jar. Neither gave in, and we ended up throwing all the jars away. What a difference a penny made! We were told not to mention this to anyone. We didn't, and now I'm the only one left who knows the story of the 1000-plus fruit jars.

Who needs TV? Speaking of North Home, it was my favorite of all the homes the hospital owned. It stood proudly on the corner of Lovell and John streets. It was a very large house with a sprawling front porch. Many a night in good weather I would sit on its porch with Mrs. Ellis or student nurses and watch people and cars traveling along Lovell Street. It was a time before TV when one could enjoy just visiting or watching, and I did a lot of both. As you entered the front door of North Home, a huge wide stairway, which divided the rooms on the east and west sides, led to the second floor. Two stairways were in the back of the house, and I remember the huge attic, which was accessible from both sides. On the first floor was the lounge and fireplace, where we had many a gab session; on the other side was the housemother's quarters, with the kitchen in back. For those who were there then, I hope you can visualize this as clearly as I can.

Bronson purchased a new nurses' residence in November 1946, located at the corner of Pine and Cedar streets—it was called East Home. Mrs. Reusch was hired as housemother. Mrs. Reusch was an ordained Methodist minister and a sister to Mrs. Ellis. Members of the Class of '48, many returning from affiliations, were moving into the newly remodeled house, which was not 100 percent completed at the time they moved in. The rest of the class remained at North Home.

In early December of that year, I pretty well knew Mrs. Wright's schedule, so I could enjoy the gab sessions in the kitchen with the class of '47, while looking out over the window at the ER entrance and staff home and not worrying about Mrs. Wright. At Christmas time we decorated the tree in the big lounge. Over at South Home

The Bronson I Knew

the class of '47 decided to have a Christmas dinner with all the trimmings.

My good friends, Jane Mayfield, Wanda Grauman, Nancy Beard, Margaret Gould and the others invited me to dinner along with Mrs. Howell, who supplied some delicious punch. I brought along my high school proofs in hope that the girls and Mrs. Howell could help me pick out the one they thought best for my high school yearbook. They couldn't agree on one picture, so I finally asked Jane Mayfield, "Will you pick out the one you like best?" She did and that picture appeared in the 1947 Kalamazoo Central yearbook. It was a great evening and I felt honored that they asked me to be a part of this special time. Mrs. Howell was so funny. I loved to hear her laugh. In the big dorm, the members of the class of '49 were all talking about capping in February and looking forward to starting on special services.

Graduation from Kalamazoo Central

In spring of '47 it started to set in that my high school days were soon coming to an end, and likewise my days working in the dorm after school. Everyone started to talk about graduation. I anticipated missing many of my close friends that I had several classes with. Most of us had the same lunch hour, and we would run across the street to Matthew's for a hamburger and hot fudge sundae. Kalamazoo Central still has a beautiful auditorium where for three years we had our assemblies and pep rallies. Our graduation exercises would occur in a couple of months. It was already May, and I needed to complete all of my assignments before graduation.

Toward the end of May, seniors received their yearbooks and ran around getting friends to sign them. We got out of school a week before the underclassmen and anxiously awaited our practice for graduation and the big night. When it arrived, we're all excited about our names being called as we marched across the stage to receive our diplomas. I went through Edison, Washington and Central with my classmate, Ken Warren, who later married Mary Proxmire, a student nurse at Bronson.

At our 20-, 25- and 50-year class reunions, I served on the planning committees. It was good to see those classmates once again, the KCHS class of '47.

It's Good to Hear from Mrs. Kirk

I have received several letters from Mrs. Kirk. I can tell that her job in New Mexico was very difficult and the weather extremely hot. She asked about the girls and how I'm getting along with the new housemother, and she sent several things that the Indians made. I loved to show them to Mrs. Wright and tell her they were from Mrs. Kirk, whom we all loved, as Mrs. Richardson and Mrs. Rinehart looked on. Mrs. Wright didn't say much, she didn't have to—her face said it all. Looking back, I guess I could have been kinder to her and, maybe in a way, it still bothers me.

Springtime Memories

Some of the things I remember from close to two years of being employed at Bronson make a lengthy list:
- The annual White Cross lawn fete on the front lawn of the hospital
- Freshman talent shows, always a big hit with many laughs
- The doctors–nurses dinner dance, which also provided many laughs, but maybe not for the doctors' wives
- Not so funny was when the trolley car at Western was not working
- Homesick girls
- Big sisters
- Cadet nurses marching to First Methodist Church
- Nicknames for doctors and some supervisors
- Hell Week
- The attic
- Starched uniforms
- Parties
- Sign-out book
- Dorm elevator
- Miss Moffat, who didn't smile
- Miss Sweet, who picked on certain girls
- Capping and black-banding

- Affiliations
- Pushing my four-wheeled cart loaded with food supplies to North and South homes during the winter months in the snow

Changes in Student Housing

On May 27, 1947, Mary B. sent a written letter to the seniors of South Home informing them that Dr. Robinson would arrive soon, to assume his duties as a surgical resident at Bronson and would move into the first floor. Also, that the laboratory students would occupy the second floor. Panic sets in as the girls were given a choice of moving next door to 426 John Street, a dark brown house, or finding an apartment for a couple of months until graduation. Mrs. Howell and Mrs. Truman, who always talked your leg off, were soon out of a job. It was hard for all of us to tell dear Mrs. Howell good-bye.

As it turned out, a month later Dr. Robinson moved into 426 John Street and a few seniors moved to the Annex. South Home returned to a nurses' residence two years later.

Dr. Machin, who arrived a few months earlier as Bronson's first resident doctor, greeted Dr. Robinson. After Mary B.'s surprising letter to the seniors at South Home, she took a leave of absence to further her graduate study on a master's of nursing degree. She planned to return in time for graduation in September.

In August of 1947, the class of '49 left for vacation—and I really hated to see them go. Before they left, they began the move to North Home with Mrs. Ellis, as members of the class of '48 left North Home and moved to East Home with Mrs. Reusch to join the rest of their classmates. Laundry carts could be seen going in both directions, and I didn't know whom to help first.

On August 25th, the class of '47 graduated. It was a rather sentimental time for me as I sat in the First Methodist Church and watched as Dr. Perdew led the processional down the aisle to the front of the church. As the graduating seniors marched by me, two by two, many memories of good times flash back. The class of '47 were freshmen in the big dorm when I started working at Bronson. They really adopted me, and will always be one of my favorite classes.

My Job Changes with the Class of 1950

As fall arrived, so did a record number of freshmen. It was the largest freshman class in the history of Bronson's nursing school—40 girls to carry in their luggage, and guess what? Most are my age. I can tell this would be a really a fun class and it wouldn't take me long to learn their names, which I did in record time—that was the good news. The sad news was that I realized it was time for me to move on and to leave a job I really loved. It was great during my high school years being "Dick the Buffer." Knowing these girls for two months was great fun and I made many friends. It would be difficult to leave, but since I had graduated from high school, I was looking for a full-time job.

I have made many friends throughout the hospital, especially Floyd Rothwell. When I informed Floyd that I was going to be looking for a new job, he said, "Dick, how would you like to work for me? The electrician quit last week and you could take his place."

"Floyd," I said, "I really don't know much about being an electrician."

He said, "If you are willing to learn, I will spend time with you and teach you the electrical trade. It's not something that you are going to learn overnight; in fact I will send homework for you to do. Are you willing to give it a try?"

I shook Floyd's hand and said I was willing to try. "Fine," he said. "Tell Granny Wright (as he called her) that you are giving her a two-week notice and that you are coming to work for me."

Saying Good-bye

Telling Mrs. Wright was easy, not so the class of '50. What fun times I had in a short time with these girls and now I would soon be telling them good-bye. Ruby Smith, the maid, and I were good friends and I always appreciated her advice, especially when it came to the girls. I knew I would miss Ruby and the good times we shared talking about the girls and whom she thought I should date. I also appreciated her covering for me when Mrs. Wright was looking for me.

Two weeks to make the rounds of North and East homes and the Annex, visiting with the girls, Mrs. Ellis and Mrs. Reusch. I know it made Mrs. Wright upset every time I told her how good Mrs. Ellis was to me, so during my last two weeks, I especially made her mad when I spent too much time at North Home. I did wax most of the students' rooms in the dorm before I left, which meant moving as much furniture as possible into the hall. Happy Lewis' room, in the northeast corner of the second floor, was the hardest of all the rooms in the dorm to do because of the shape of the room, which meant I couldn't get much furniture into the hall.

Those two weeks flew by so fast. I'll never forget my last day. I sort of had a sick feeling that morning riding my bike to work, knowing I would be telling the girls good-bye and how much I would miss them. The good news I had for them was that my good friend, Bill Brush, would be taking my job. They would find Bill a lot of fun to be around, and I was happy to recommend him as my replacement. Bill was a senior at Kalamazoo Central so he would be around for awhile. Near the end of the day, the girls and Ruby called me into Room 307, a large room on the third floor. They presented me with a sterling bracelet inscribed on the back, "From Ruby and the Class of '50." (Now I realize why they couldn't afford to publish a *White Caps* yearbook!) After thanking them and sharing a few hugs, I said my farewells, rode the elevator to the first floor and decided to ring the man bell, which I thought would be the last time. I gave my key to Mrs. Wright, and said good-bye to her, took one last look around and rode my bike toward home, with maybe a tear or two in my eyes and feeling depressed.

Riding past Upjohn Park I stopped for a few minutes and thought back to my short time working in the lab for Dr. Prentice. How thankful I was to leave the rabbits and guinea pigs. And now I had a real hurt feeling, knowing I no longer had a job I really loved and the girls I left behind. So ended another chapter in my life at Bronson.

~

The Bronson I Knew

4
BECOMING AN ELECTRICIAN DURING HOSPITAL EXPANSION IN THE LATE 1940s

I had mixed emotions as I rode my bike to work Monday morning. I hadn't slept too much over the weekend, asking myself what did I know about electricity and what would be the reaction of the employees? Now as I approached the hospital, those same thoughts were still with me. I parked my bike in the same place as usual and punched in. I walked past the cafeteria and said hi to several girls, which helped put a smile on my face.

Orientation to Electrical Work

Floyd was in his office waiting for me. "How's my electrician?" he beamed.

"OK," I said, not too sure of myself.

"Here, let me give you my own electric tool pouch with a few tools in it," he said, "and you will need to buy several others—by the way, did I tell you what your working hours are?"

"No," I said, "you just said to be here at 7:00 A.M."

He lit his cigar and said, "We work 7:00 A.M. to 4:30 P.M., with a half hour for lunch. You are to work every other Saturday and every other holiday." That didn't sound too bad, especially working every other holiday, which meant he expected me to be around for awhile.

"Put on your tool pouch and I'll show you the maintenance shop." We walked up the back stairwell and out the back entrance.

Great Scot, I thought, I hope it's not near those rabbits and pigs! It wasn't, but there were three small sheds in the vicinity of the Guild House, and around the corner from them and directly behind the Staff Home was a three-car garage. Floyd said, "Welcome to the Maintenance Department, Dick."

Inside the garage, or the shop as it was called, were Roy VandenBerg and Ralph Stewart. Roy was the carpenter and Ralph was the mechanic. I knew them both from the lunchroom. Even thought they both greeted me warmly, I'm sure they wondered how I was going to work out—a kid of 18 replacing Marcus, a licensed electrician. After Floyd showed me my work area and after maybe an hour of small talk between the four of us, Floyd and I left for his office. Passing by the three sheds I said, "Floyd, what are these sheds used for?"

He said, "Do you really want to know? Well, the first one is where Mac the yardman keeps his equipment—the second is where Lyle from surgery throws things left over from surgery, and the last one is where the kitchen garbage is dumped." He continued to say, "At 6:00 A.M. every morning, Jake comes with his pickup truck and shovels everything into his truck and heads for the dump."

I wanted to say, "I think he missed a few rats," but I didn't. Looking back, it's hard to believe that it was the way we disposed of things.

Light Bulb Duty

Back at Floyd's office, he showed me where the electric bulbs were stored. A box about 15 inches square contained a variety of light bulbs. Floyd said, "Dick, the first thing you are to do is take this box of bulbs and replace any that are burned out. Start on the sixth floor and work your way to the basement." On my maiden voyage, Floyd went with me. On Hall 5 I met Mrs. Stell, who gave me a quick hello and good-bye. Next we went through surgery, which I found to be a little scary, with patients on carts and doctors and nurses buzzing around. I was glad to meet Miss Wolters and get the heck out of there without having to replace any burned out lights. OB floor was quiet with only babies crying in the nursery. Miss Wantz, whom I had seen before when waxing Mary B's car, said hi to me and left with a doctor. As we moved to the second floor, I saw for the first time the men and women's wards, which I remember the nurses talking about. On the same floor was Peds and at the end of the hall was 2 West, where I had been a patient. I enjoyed seeing Mrs. Maxwell again.

So far, I had only replaced two light bulbs, which with my height I could reach without a ladder. As we moved to Hall 1, I saw an old friend, Shirley Evans, who always had a smile. She greeted me warmly. Our last stop was through the kitchen, where I said hello to Mrs. Stuteville, the dietician, and then to x-ray and Herman Heystek. Finally we went through the lab which I was more than familiar with—thank goodness, no Dr. Prentice!

Learning the Routine

We returned to Floyd's office, and he told me to go to the shop where he would be shortly. It was 9:00 A.M. when I returned, to find Roy and Ralph still sitting at their benches. So not knowing what to do, I sat with them. After quite awhile, Floyd made his appearance and he sat with us. No one seemed to be in a hurry, and I wondered if this was to be our daily routine.

It's late fall of 1947, and there we sat—the engineer, carpenter, mechanic and me—we were the Maintenance Department along with Forrest, the painter, who was probably sitting in his little paint shop next to the pigs and rabbits. Once the guys had all the world's problems solved, Floyd and I would head for the laundry to see Harvey Meyers. He was a stern man, who never smiled. One of my jobs was to lubricate all the equipment in the laundry. Harvey ran a tight ship. None of his employees dared to chat while working, which I knew about from my days in the dorm, but as time went by, and Harvey wasn't watching, I managed to talk with Blanche, the redheaded seamstress.

Around 11:30 A.M. we headed to wash up for lunch, using the small bathroom next to Floyd's office. Jack Tribe, Bill Van Haaften and Amos Eash, from housekeeping, found us as we sat on the long bench in Floyd's office. At the stroke of 11:45 A.M., we all headed for lunch—a routine we followed for several years.

In the afternoon I learned to repair the nurse call cords, using a test panel that Floyd had made. I tested call cords and arranged my work area until 4:30 P.M. when it was time to go home. We padlocked the shop, and I headed for home as I wondered *what* the future held for me as the hospital electrician.

During the first few weeks, I learned where all the fuse panels were located; repaired some small electrical equipment; studied a book on electricity, which Floyd always reviewed with me; and had time to wander around the hospital. My wandering always found me at North Home for a visit with Mrs. Ellis and, of course, I managed to change a light bulb or two. I loved to venture up to the attic in North Home where there were many items left, from who knows where and how long ago. There was a unique desk that I would check on every time I was up there. It was a prize possession that I would have liked to own.

That first week I learned that, even though our hospital was small, the three of us would be required to help each other many times. For me, it would prove to be a godsend. On many occasions Ralph and Roy willingly helped me out, since they both had a basic knowledge of electricity. I had a chance to return the favor when Bronson rented three large classrooms on the third floor of the Harding School from the Kalamazoo Public Schools. Because Harding had no elevators, the three of us had to carry those heavy hospital beds and bedside cabinets, etc., up three flights of stairs. It took us about a week to get the job done, with Miss Sweet looking over our shoulders. We had to be careful since Harding School was still being used for teaching elementary students. Looking back, I think carrying those heavy beds contributed to my back problems. On the positive side, the freshmen class could be seen every morning, walking from the back of the dorm to Harding School. I always just happened to be in that area when they went by, causing one or two to be a little late for class.

In looking back, for the class of 1950 and me, Harding School holds many memories. With no elevator, we often wondered if Miss Sweet had the energy to teach after climbing three flights of stairs; and with no air conditioning, the classrooms were very hot. The school's bell rang every 50 minutes as the elementary students changed classes to disturb the girls' concentration. In the winter the cold air blew through the frosted windows, and the "frozen" girls couldn't wait to get back to the dorm and their warm rooms.

Week-ends and Holidays

I looked forward to the Saturdays I worked so I could have lunch with Bill Brush. As one might imagine, we had discussions about the girls and I could tell Bill was enjoying his job. We talked about the girls whom we would like to date. Since neither of us had a car, our dates were to the movies or football games. Bill and I went to the same church, so after the night services, we would walk over to the hospital and wander around the basement area in hopes of seeing some student nurses. We usually ended up in the boiler room talking to the night fireman. Big disappointment!

Thanksgiving was my first holiday to work. Roy and I always worked the holidays together as a pair, and Ralph and Floyd made the alternate pair. There was not much to do; we were basically there for emergencies. I listened and learned much from Roy whom I really liked and appreciated. We sat in the shop and kept warm sitting next to the radiator. From time to time, I would venture over to Floyd's office to see if anyone had brought a maintenance work order down, and maybe make my way up to the floors to see whomever was working.

We always left our jackets in the hall across from the one-room Emergency Room. We never seemed to lose anything, except the one time I wore my Eisenhower jacket and left it where we always did. It was gone when we came back, and I felt bad about it. My brother-in-law had given it to me when he returned from Europe after the war, so after that incident, we carried our jackets into Floyd's office and left them there.

Christmas Vacation for Bill

Christmas time meant that Bill Brush was on a two-week vacation from school. I could hardly wait to see him. We could eat lunch together and compare notes on the girls. What a fun two weeks we had. He let me run my old buffer on the third floor as Ruby looked on. Since Granny Wright was on a week's vacation at her home in East Lansing, we sat in the girls' rooms and laughed and joked with them. It turned out to be a great Christmas with Bill, the girls and Ruby, plus all the candy, nuts and parties.

We Were Small, but Dedicated

The hospital was still small in 1947—there were about 200 employees. Most of us knew each other by name, especially the ones we wanted to know. Housekeeping had three janitors and six maids; laundry consisted of two men and ten women; and maintenance had an engineer, carpenter, mechanic, painter, yardman, three boiler operators and myself. In those days almost all employees were underpaid, working nine hours a day, six days a week. But then as Dr. Perdew reminded us—we were special people whose dedication to humanity was our reward and somehow, back then, that sounded convincing.

My contacts with Dr. Perdew in my early years were far and few between. I guess he knew who I was since, when he saw me, he always said, "Hello Dick." I guess it was Mary B. who told him who I was. Lucky for me I didn't have to do any electrical work in his office. Only once did I change a light bulb over his desk, and that's when he asked me how I liked working at Bronson.

"I really like it," I said, and could have said (but didn't), "I really like the student nurses too!"

Cold Winter in Maintenance

The winter months in the maintenance shop were always cold; in fact, very cold. The three of us spent much time there, and kept our jackets on most of the day just to keep warm. The thinly constructed garage was no match for the cold north wind. When I got too cold, I would venture down to the boiler room to warm up and chat with Jim Pearson, the day fireman.

Every morning, Floyd and I would go over the homework he had given me to do. I can't begin to say how much time he devoted to my education. I will always be indebted to that wonderful man and his patience with me.

Bronson as a Family Place

In the middle to late '40s, Maxine Ketchum Clark, her brother Karyle, her mother and stepfather all worked in the kitchen at Bronson. You might say it was a family affair. Maxine and Karyle were both employed there for over 35 years. It was not uncommon for several members of a family to be employed at Bronson. Junior and

Debbie Ashby and several members of their family worked at Bronson, as did many family units, as I can later testify to, concerning the Vander Molen clan.

One employee, who worked in the kitchen, was known affectionately as Peg-Leg Louie. He was a friend to everyone, a happy-go-lucky kind of guy. Louie was a man who thought you could cure any ailment with his brand of herbs, which he prepackaged in capsule form. He was always asking me how I was feeling and I told him, "I feel great, Louie."

Then one day I didn't feel very well, and Louie said to me, "Dick, I have just the thing for you. Take this pill with a glass of water and you will feel better." He was such a nice guy and I didn't want to hurt his feelings, so I took the capsule while he watched. I didn't feel any different for the first 15 minutes, but shortly after that my stomach started to burn; in fact, I drank another glass of cold water and told Louie that my stomach was on fire. His comment was, "Good, it's working." After a few more glasses of water the burning stopped and I forgot about not feeling well. It was the last time that I took Louie's herb pills, even if he was a nice guy. When I told Floyd about it he laughed and said, "Let that be a lesson to you, Dick."

As we began 1948, Bill went back to school and I was feeling a little depressed. All the talk in the cafeteria was about the expansion of the hospital. We heard that construction might begin in summer. I became a good friend of Dr. Herbert, who came to the maintenance shop for an extension cord and found out that we had something in common—namely, the Detroit Tigers. He and Dr. Robinson began their surgical residency the previous July. I wondered why it took Dr. Herbert so long to find me.

As February rolled around, the class of '50 was excited about black-banding. Evelyn, the cook, prepared the meals in the kitchen and Miss Noble, the purchasing agent, was giving out only six thumbtacks at a time, no more. It was beginning to be a joke—as you could only have two pencils and no more, it was the same with all the other items she controlled. Mrs. Stell on Hall 6 told me not to talk with the students when I was on her floor. I was still frightened of her, so I didn't, but life goes on.

Howard City, Here We Come

It was 7:00 A.M. on a wintry Sunday morning in February 1948. I tried to start my brother Andy's car. Finally, after several tries, it turned over and I was on my way to pick up Shirley Motyer and Tomo Hamamura at the big dorm. When I arrived, they were standing at the front door and came running when they saw me. I said, "Hi girls, keep your coats on, it's as cold in here as it is outside." We were headed for Howard City to pick up Gwen Motyer, Shirley's older sister, who was a junior student at Bronson, and a roommate of Tomo. Shirley was in her freshman year at Bronson. Gwen had been home for several days, and because she and Shirley wanted to bring several things back to Bronson, I agreed to drive to Howard City and pick up Gwen, along with whatever they wanted to bring back.

When we arrived in Howard City, Mrs. Motyer and Derwin, Gwen and Shirley's younger brother, greeted us. After lunch and with the temperature still below zero, we headed back to Kalamazoo. Derwin later became a Bronson employee. Mrs. Motyer became a good friend of Boop and me, and whenever we went north, we stopped for a visit with her. The trip to Howard City was one of many that I, or Boop and I, made for the girls who needed rides to their homes or elsewhere.

I should have mentioned this before, but it was always tough to see student nurses fail after several months of study. It was the same with every class. Girls would lose a roommate and we would lose a friend. It was a happy time for all those who made it, but our hurt was for those who didn't.

Finishing Jack's Job

Previously I mentioned that Jack Tribe and I started washing walls in the big dorm, but due to Jack's problems, we never finished. Mary B. approached me one day in March and asked if I would be willing to help Bill finish washing the walls in the girl's rooms. We would do it in the evenings after we had finished with our regular jobs. It sounded great to me; in fact, I was elated to be back in the dorm and also to see the girls. But first I asked Floyd if it was OK with him. Floyd said, "No problem, Dick, just don't fall off the ladder."

Bill and I had a picnic. It was more fun than work. As we kidded with the girls, we were always aware that Granny Wright might make her appearance. I'm sure the girls whose room we were washing didn't get much studying done. It was a time that Bill and I reminisced about for years.

Hospital Expansion

"It's never going to be the same," I tell myself as I watched Bishop Raymond J. Wade break ground in back of the hospital on May 19, 1948. The expansion, which was talked about, planned, and designed, began as a crowd gathered to watch. Floyd and I watched from the roof of the sixth floor. It was the beginning of the end of the small hospital that we knew. As the construction crew moved in, many changes were taking place. No more could we walk out of the back of the dorm to the ER entrance. Also, the horseshoe entrance and the garden area would be gone. G. Ray Hall had to bring his ambulance patients to the front entrance, as did the vendors, at least on a temporary basis. The patients could hear the sound of the heavy earth-moving equipment, the carpenters' hammers and the whining of the saws. It was the first phase of Bronson's expansion—the service building. The laundry, general storeroom, and housekeeping office would be located on the ground floor. What was a joy to Roy, Ralph and me was that the Maintenance Department would move to the old laundry area. No more freezing in the garage. I should add that the big dorm would be right above us. The second floor would include two large nursing school classrooms—no

The Bronson I Knew

more walking up three flights of stairs for Miss Sweet—and a White Cross workroom. On the third floor would be a children's playroom.

When I had spare time, I would watch with interest as construction proceeded, many times from the kitchen on the third floor of the dorm with Ruby. One had to feel sorry, not only for the patients during this time, but also for the maids who had a hard time with all of the dust. I should mention that my other favorite spot to watch construction was the penthouse above the sixth floor. I had to check on several motors in this area, and I always found time to watch the progress below. Also, from my vantage point, I could see my house on Carr Street.

With the construction going on, I almost forgot that Bill had graduated from Kalamazoo Central and was now working in the dorm. He and I are the two youngest employees, along with a few nurses' aides. We would arrange to meet them for lunch whenever we could. One of the girls lived at Long Lake, so Bill and I decided to hitch hike to her house for a swim. We not only had to walk most of the way, but we didn't find her house either. After a cooling swim at Summer Home Park, we headed home. I remember it well—the long walk, that is.

After that we turned our attention back to the student nurses. Double dating with the students at the movies or playing tennis at Upjohn Park were fun times during the summer months. Whenever Bill found out that Granny Wright had gone shopping, he would make his way over to the shop and pay me a visit. I often had a Tiger ballgame on the radio so we would listen to a few innings before he left for the dorm.

Class of 1951 and Boop

In July we began seeing strings of safety pins dangling from the uniforms of the class of 1948. Each day they would remove one pin until the commencement day on August 16th. The class of 1948 was the last Cadet class to enter Bronson. With them went the memories of my stab wound and the stuck elevator. More important was that a new class would be arriving on September 12th. Forty-two girls in all—and one of these girls will become *my wife*, but I didn't know that yet, nor did she, as I carried her luggage to the four-bed room on the third floor across from the elevator. Her three roommates, I learned, were all from Grand Rapids. I didn't spend much time talking as I had more girls to see and more luggage to carry. "These girls are good-lookers," I say to myself, "and why couldn't Bill be around today to help me so we could compare notes."

Out-foxed by Granny . . . Bill had decided to take a few courses at Western and would have to wait until Monday to realize what he had missed. This is again the largest class to enter Bronson so it's going to take me awhile to know them all, especially if Granny Wright has anything to do with it. I noticed that many of the girls have boyfriends who don't seem to want to leave. I tell myself, "Enjoy yourselves today, boys, for tomorrow they are mine and Bill's." I made sure that when the class of 1950 moved to East Home, they took all the extension cords with them, so guess what? I would then need to come over on Monday to see what needed to be hooked up and how many extension cords were needed.

On Monday afternoon when I finally got over to the big dorm, it was mass confusion with the 42 girls. I said hi to a few of them, told them I am "Dick, the electrician," and that I would be back later in the week to see if they needed anything. Of course, I knew they would.

I waited until Thursday before I went back, knowing that by then almost everyone would need an extension cord and that I should be in great demand, or so I hoped. Granny heard me ring the man bell, and it wasn't long before she was hot on my trail. Rather sheepishly, I told her, "Those juniors took all the extension cords to East Home with them, and would you like me to hook up desk lamps, etc., for the girls?"

I thought I had her over a barrel, but she said, "*I* will check with the girls to see what they need and *I* will let you know."

Big deal, I thought, is she going to hook them up too? I needed to know the name of the blond and brunette I had seen earlier. It really bugged me to be outfoxed by Granny. I told Bill about my dilemma, and he thought it was funny.

"I have the solution," Ruby told me on the phone. "Come up when Granny is down for lunch at 12:30." I did, but to my dismay, the girls were away at Western. Some solution—but Ruby and I had a good talk anyway. These students were 18 years old, and I needed to know them with or without Granny's help.

After a few days I received two pages of requests for extension cords and light bulbs, with the rooms listed. "Thanks, Granny," I said to myself, as I set about getting acquainted with the class of 1951.

Meanwhile, construction workers put in long hours on the construction of the service building. They hoped to finish the construction by December, and it was on schedule. Floyd and I toured the new building almost every day, as a good education for me to see all the construction trade people doing their work. It also gave me an opportunity to locate the electrical service boxes and panels. I would need to know where they were located when the building was completed.

My First Car

I had purchased a 1937 Pontiac Coupe, and dated several girls. None happened to be my future wife. However, I saw a blond when she arrived that September day. She was one of the girls from Grand Rapids who was a roommate of Betty Gosling, the student nurse who would become my wife. I also became good friends with a brunette, as well as others in the class of 1951.

Looking back, I remember that shortly after I bought my car, Bill and I took a week's vacation. We drove to Cadillac, then to the Thumb Area and ended up in Detroit to see a night Tiger baseball game. Only a few night games were played that year. We also called on a nurse who had left training in her freshman year. We had enough money for one night in a hotel, so the first night we slept in the car on a side street in Detroit. I don't think we had much sleep that night. The second night, after the game, we went to a hotel so we could shower. After the game we headed home broke, but glad we had gone.

Just to let you know, I haven't forgotten the girls at North and East homes. I would take them to the bus station, to Ruby's house at Austin Lake, to Grand Rapids or beyond, to Woods Lake and Long Lake. I tried to touch all my bases. Even then I considered myself to be a friend of the student nurses, or at least that's the way I would like to be remembered.

Christmas and Chocolates

Christmas at Bronson was lonely without my good friend, Bill. Bill had started a new job in early December and I really missed him. We spent many happy hours playing tricks on the girls.

The cafeteria was decorated for Christmas when some of the best meals were served that week. Dietary was kind enough not to serve hash during the holiday season, but I'm sure they made up for it later. The employee Christmas parties were held in the sixth floor auditorium, with a speech from Dr. Perdew. Then we were all given a one-pound box of chocolates from the Chocolate Shop. Department heads were given a two-pound box of chocolates. Christmas time was the best of times at Bronson.

Moving to New Quarters

In January 1949 the service building was completed. Mr. S.A. Lott, administrative resident, was charged with the move to new quarters. The School of Nursing enjoyed their two new, large classrooms. Miss Sweet, the Nursing Arts instructor, and her two assistants, Joan Kiewiet and Virginia McPhail had no more steps to climb. Ray Hall could once again bring his patients directly to the Emergency Room. We in the maintenance shop began the move to our new quarters in the vacated laundry area. It proved to be a good location, especially for me, to see the girls coming and going to classes as well as to the cafeteria. Forrest, the painter, moved in with us since the Guild House, the three sheds, and our old shop will soon come down as the expansion continued. A large dumpster was now used for garbage and for surgery to dispose its various items.

Mrs. Martha Beatty became the new social director for the School of Nursing and it was only a matter of time before we clashed. From some of the girls, I found out she was upset that I was dating the students. I did not go to college. She told the girls they should only go out with college guys. She rarely spoke to me and, for the time being, I said nothing to her.

The Oaks

In spring of 1949, during construction of the main six-story hospital, the two beautiful oak trees on the front lawn had to be cut down. In the nurses' yearbook of 1947, they wrote about those beautiful oak trees:

> ***THE OAKS***
> Of distinctive beauty are the huge oaks gracing the front lawn of Bronson Methodist Hospital. To patients, nurses, visitors and casual passers-by these oaks have become beloved landmarks.
>
> Seasons have come and gone, but the oaks remained through historical decades. As tiny saplings, they had their beginnings during Indian days. Titus Bronson passed them, no doubt, when he was establishing his trading post. When much larger, their welcome shade beckoned a settler to build his farmhouse nearby. They were of imposing height in 1900, when the hospital opened its doors to a dozen patients. Seven years ago, they become more beautiful and impressive, silhouetted against the brick backdrop of the new building.

> To make room for a greater Bronson, the oaks must come down. Their beauty, however, will not be completely destroyed, but rather translated indoors. Fashioned from their wood, the altar of the new Memorial Chapel will be of distinctive beauty, and like them, a symbol of strength, dignity and hope for all.

So much happened during spring and summer of 1949. Dr. May and Dr. Warren Patow joined Bronson's resident staff. It didn't take Dr. May long to find George Todd, the 11:00 P.M. to 7:00 A.M. fireman, who loved to fish. They could be seen catching night crawlers on the front lawn of the hospital. George took Dr. May under his wing, and they fished whenever possible.

Boop

The other really big news was that I started dating Betty Lou Gosling. Known to her friends as Boop, a name she tells me was given to her by her Uncle Dwight, from the comic strip, "Betty Boop." She was a beautiful girl with long brown hair and sparkling blue eyes. After a few dates, I took her home to meet my family. I had told my sister that this was the girl I really liked. No longer did I care to date other girls. Not long after, her classmates knew that we were going steady. Mrs. Beatty also heard that I was dating Boop. She told her she could do better and should meet someone from Western Michigan

College or Kalamazoo College. Boop was hurt and didn't tell me, but her roommate, Marty, did. I talked with Floyd, who had been like a father to me. He had already met Boop and thought she was great, so he advised me to confront Mrs. Beatty, which I did.

Mrs. Beatty was sitting at her desk. She looked up as I came in, and said, "Is there something you want?"

As I banged my fist on her desk, I said, "Yes there is—who do you think you are to tell Betty Gosling not to date me, and that I'm not good enough for her? Do you understand I could sue you for defaming my character? Is it in your job description to advise the girls as to who they can and can't date? I intend to tell Miss Anderson about this, and don't you ever dare interfere with us again."

She said nothing, I think she was so scared that she couldn't. When I left her office quite a crowd had gathered in the hall to listen in. Several girls patted me on the back as I left.

I did go see Miss Anderson at her office. Mary B., I always felt, liked me, so I felt comfortable telling her about Mrs. Beatty. "Don't worry, Dick," she said, "I will take care of it," and she did.

Mrs. Beatty called Floyd, and asked to see me. This time when I went to her office, it was my turn to say, "Is there something you want?"

"Yes," she said, "I want to apologize to you and Betty and I'm sorry for what I said." Thank you, Mary B.—you came through for me again, I thought.

I did say, "Thank you," and left.

Granny must have heard about it too, because she invited me to her apartment for a cold glass of punch and casually mentioned it. Could this be a start of a new friendship and my freedom to the dorm and maybe to the room that housed four girls from Grand Rapids?

Joining the Naval Reserve

About six or seven of us guys from First Reformed Church decided, sometime after graduation from high school, to join the Naval Reserve. The Navy had built a new building on Lake Street, and we would be required to attend meetings every Monday night for four years and take two-week cruises each year. America was at peace and we could get paid—we all thought it was a good idea. Many times after the Monday meeting we would go out for coffee. After listening to Bill and me talk about the nurses, the guys asked if I could get them dates. I said kiddingly, "It won't be easy, but I'll try." As a matchmaker I did all right. Three of the guys married the girls that I had lined up for them.

A Bronson Patient Again

In the middle of August, Boop and I were on a double date with John Bowers and Marty Martin, Boop's roommate, where I had played the role of matchmaker. I wasn't feeling well, and thought it was the hot weather. As the evening wore on, they decided I should go to the Emergency Room. I was admitted to the hospital with double pneumonia, and stayed for five days. This was beginning to be a habit! Little did I know this wouldn't be the last time that I would become a patient, but how I loved those twice-a-day back rubs. Those student nurses sure received good training!

Polio Ward

As we all watched the oak trees come down and the cornerstone laid for the new hospital building and medical center, our attention soon turned to the polio outbreak in Kalamazoo. Miss Adriana VanBoven was put in charge of Hall 1, as it turned into the polio ward. All of us became involved in one way or another. For me, it meant installing the nurse call-cord inside the iron lung for the patient who was inside. While feeling sad for the patient inside the iron lung, I could smell the moist woolen pads long after I would leave the floor. Student nurses were heating the woolen packs in hot water and wringing them out before application. They used an old-fashioned wringer in the long and narrow utility room that you could hardly turn around in. For those of us who worked in the polio ward, we will never forget the patients that we came to know and love.

Remember us for . . . On a happy note, for the class of 1949, came graduation. This class had spent their last two years at North Home with Mrs. Ellis, except for two months at Sigma Gamma in Mount Clemens and three months at State Hospital. They will always be remembered for the fact that they had no money and no yearbook, but they always sent really nice cards to those who were sick or celebrating a special event.

On Wednesday, July 15th, North Home was to be moved to Pine Street and become Pine Home. This move was to be completed on Thursday morning. However, the movers didn't realize how heavy the North Home was, with its three fireplaces. It took several days to move, blocking Lovell Street the whole time. East Home was also renamed as Cedar Home. Mrs. Ellis and Mrs. Reusch are now neighbors as these houses are all connected.

Farewell to 1940s Classes and Welcome 1950s

The nursing classes of the forties took some of these memories with them:

- The Derby Inn across from North Home
- Joldersma and Klein Funeral Home on the corner of Lovell and Henrietta streets
- The Capitol, State and Fuller Theatres
- The famous Kewpee hamburgers and frosty shakes

In September we said our farewells to the class of 1949 and I helped move the class of 1952 into the dorm. It became more of a tradition for me because I had already found "my" nurse. I continued to supply the girls with extension cords and lights, fix their small appliances, and learn their names.

The way it was . . . Morale was high during the 1940s, and patient care couldn't have been better. You could stay in the hospital until you were well enough to go home or you were permitted to die in the hospital. Nurses wore white uniforms with caps and stood when doctors appeared at the nursing stations. Doctors still carried their medical bags and made rounds. Nurse aides wore green uniforms.

Perceived Staff Jobs

In November, the hospital hired Warren Von Ehren as assistant superintendent to Dr. Perdew, to be in charge of professional and special services, while Karl Gibson continued in charge of finances. This allowed Dr. Perdew to spend more time on the construction project.

Subtitles only . . . His name was Howard, and he was the relief fireman. His hobby was making home movies. For several months he took movies of employees at work—in the laundry, housekeeping, dietary and Maintenance Department—to be shown at our Christmas Party held in the sixth floor auditorium. We were all anxious to see Howard's movie. Dr. Perdew and Mary B. were in attendance, the lights were turned out and the movie began. No sound—only subtitles. We all laughed at the pictures and especially at the subtitles. Jack Tribe was shown washing the windows and was listed as a member of the Lost Tribe; Roy VandenBerg, as a nice guy; Ada Reimer, as Mother May, etc. And then there was the picture of me, and it said, "Dick, the hospital stud." The crowd yelled. I don't know what Dr. Perdew and Mary B. did, but I felt my face get beet red. I think it was still red when the lights came on and I felt everyone looking at me. Looking back, I think I was the first one to leave the auditorium before anyone could ask me any questions.

The Maintenance Shop

The maintenance shop became well-established in the former area of the laundry. The three of us staked out the areas that we each would like. Roy and Ralph had the south area of the shop, while I chose a small room to work in and to store the electrical supplies. It was our first winter in the new area. We did not complain that year, because the new area was warm and comfortable.

Floyd remained in his office by the boiler room. Forrest, the painter, also had a corner of the shop. In our new location we no longer met in Floyd's office for lunch because the cafeteria was close to the shop. The morgue, in case I forgot to mention it, was located just before the cafeteria, when coming from the dorm. On occasion Dr. Prentice performed an autopsy, just when *liver* was on the lunch menu. Twice, Dr. Prentice asked me to help her put a body on the morgue table as she was by herself, and I happened to be walking by. I didn't dare say no, but it bothered me to touch a dead body. Thankfully, it was covered.

Who needs money? Miss Anderson once called the maintenance shop at telephone number 317 to ask if Bill Brush and I would be willing to do some work for her at Wall Lake. She owned a cottage and wanted to open it up for the year. We said, "Yes," and followed her in her car to Wall Lake on a Friday afternoon. She also took along Miss Wantz and Miss Wolters. While Miss Wolters was preparing dinner, Bill and I started to wash windows. Miss Anderson, who loved to fish, was down at the dock checking out her rowboat.

After a large dinner, Bill and I did some yard work, and then spent the night on the porch trying to sleep. Most of the time, however, we spent laughing and telling each other stories about the nurses. Saturday, after breakfast, we worked until noon and then Miss Anderson said, "Good job, boys, you can leave now. Thank you for your help."

On the way home Bill said, "I guess that dinner and breakfast was our pay." And so it was.

Maintenance and Housekeeping Picnic

During the long, hot summer, with no air-conditioning in the hospital, I thought it would be a good idea if the maintenance and housekeeping departments had a picnic at Milham Park. I didn't think we needed to ask administration for permission, which I attribute to my youth. I set the date and told the guys and gals we would meet for lunch at 1:00 P.M. and they were to bring a dish to pass. Floyd and Ada Reimer, our two bosses were all for it. I also told everyone not to punch out, as we deserved to be paid for the afternoon. I can't believe I did that. Anyway, we had a great time, good food, played Bingo and enjoyed the zoo. I guess we were not missed, as we never heard about our day out at the park. By the way—we never did it again!

On another occasion, I remember the business office staff going to Milham Park after work for a hamburger fry with side dishes to pass. One guy was bringing the hamburgers, but there was a problem—rumor had it that he stopped off for a drink and forgot to show up. Needless to say, that picnic was a flop and the hamburger guy never lived it down. At least they had the side dishes to eat and didn't go hungry.

Looking for Boop

The class of 1951 was now enjoying their new home on Pine Street, with Mrs. Ellis in charge. Their new large recreation room contained a ping-pong table, a jukebox and a place to hold dances. I became a regular visitor to the apartment of Mrs. Ellis, who was always glad to see me with my grapevine news. Little did she suspect that I was really looking for Boop. On one of my visits I ventured up to the attic to check on the valuable desk, only to find that it had disappeared, possibly during the move from Lovell Street.

At Christmas, Boop and I drove to Grand Rapids so I could meet her folks. Her 16-year-old sister, Shirley, was still home, and her brother and his fiancée joined us.

Boop did not tell them we were going steady, I think she was afraid of what her dad might say.

As I drove home alone on that Christmas night, I knew that I was in love with the most wonderful girl in the world, and couldn't wait for her three-day vacation to end. We had arranged earlier that at the end of the vacation, I would pick her up and bring her back to the dorm. As we drove out of her folks' driveway for the trip back to Kalamazoo, the first words out of my mouth were, "What did your folks say about me?" Her mother thought I was nice but awfully thin, and her dad said, "Please don't get serious, but spend more of your time studying."

I interpreted this to mean, "See less of this guy." That's not exactly what I wanted to hear, I said to myself. We turned our attention to other things and had a great time talking, as we parked the car in front of Pine Home.

Several of the girls and their dates were already on the porch saying good night with a kiss or two, as we joined in. Mother Ellis, as usual, turned on the porch light and said, "Girls, its time to come in." It was an every night ritual. As I left for home I was reassured that our love for each other was stronger than her dad's advice.

What's next, Mabel? Earlier, I mentioned Mrs. Stell. She always seemed to know when I was on her floor. She kept track of me as thoroughly as Granny Wright did. Mrs. Stevenson, a nurse's aide on Hall 5, came to Floyd's office to exchange batteries and light bulbs when the bad ones were brought in. Mrs. Stevenson, whom I liked, exchanged these items many times. On one particular day when Mrs. Stevenson came, I happened to mention that Hall 5 seemed to be using more batteries than the other floors.

The next thing I knew, I was being called to Mr. Gibson's office to explain why I was accusing Mrs. Stell of stealing batteries. How could she do that? I thought. I had always felt that she didn't like me, but to try and get me in trouble was quite another thing. Mr. Gibson, who was Floyd's boss, was very understanding when I told him what I had said. He seemed to be more interested in talking about the new building than Mrs. Stell. As I left his office I had almost forgotten what I was there for. I surely didn't know it then, and would not have believed it, but someday I would be calling Mrs. Stell, "Mabel," and we would become good friends.

~

Clockwise from left: My Christmas with Jiggs, late 1930s; with my father, Abraham Vander Molen, in our backyard off Carr St., ca 1943; on my bike in the front of our Carr St. home.

Early Photo History

Crew in the Bronson maintenance shed shop.

Back entrance to hospital also shows G. Ray Hall ambulance (rear door open), sheds and maintenance shop, Guild House and staff House.

At age 15, I'm on my bike, ready to go to work at Bronson.

The Vander Molen siblings, early 1950s, left to right: *back row* Andy, Dick, Jim; *middle row* Elsie, Alice, Gertrude; *front row* Florence, Esther, Evelyn.

Early Photo History

Clockwise from left: Sitting at a nurse's desk in the smoking room at the big dorm when I was 15; Herman Backert; my 1947 graduation from Kalamazoo Central High School; relaxing with Bill Brush (on the right) at the back of the hospital, 1948.

Housemothers, left to right: Mrs. Ellis, Mrs. Reusch, Mrs. Wright, and Mrs. Howell.

The big dorm, later known as Wesley Hall.

6
A NEW HOSPITAL AND A NEW LIFE

With the medical center nearing completion during the spring of 1950, a special enclosed wooden ramp was built from the front entrance of the hospital to a temporary entrance in back of the medical center. This would necessarily be used for two to three months because the business office and administration would soon be moving to their new location on the first floor. Meanwhile, the second and third floors of the medical center were being completed. It proved to be a fairly steep ramp, and we were all glad when it was no longer needed. Only four or five minor accidents happened while the ramp was in use.

Finally, the day arrived that we all had been waiting for—the opening of the medical center. It was the first of its kind in Kalamazoo. It housed many of the following doctors: Appel and Appel, Bennett and Bennett, Peelen and VanderVelde, Betz and DePree, Conrad and Hanson, Heersma and Dew, Hoebeke and Birch, Hubbel and Kilgore, Marshall and Finton, Martens and Lavender, Roger Scholten, Martin Patmos, and Paul Schrier. Most important to me was the snack bar; to others, the pharmacy; and to the student nurses, the chapel. Construction continued as the six-floor main addition began to show above ground level.

Good-bye and Hello

In July Mary B. decided it was time to say good-bye to Granny Wright. It caught most of us by surprise. I'm sure it did to Granny too. Before she left, she called maintenance and asked to see me. We sat in her office for almost an hour, reminiscing about her years at Bronson. I asked her what she was going to do. She told me she had a home in East Lansing and would spend her retirement there. When I left, we shook hands and she asked me to please come see her. I did not know that at the death of a housemother years later, I would see her again—at her home.

When Mrs. Richardson and Mrs. Rinehart retired, Mrs. Harriet Irwin and Mrs. Holcome replaced them. Mrs. Holcome was the maid on the second floor, and every Wednesday she handed out the towels and linens for the week from a locked closet in the hall. Since I knew where the key was hidden, the girls sometimes asked me to get them an extra towel and wash cloth, which I did. Luckily no one ever knew. Mrs. Irwin was the maid on the first floor, and was liked by all of the nurses, so it came as no surprise that she replaced Mrs. Wright as housemother. She was there to greet the 49 girls from the class of 1953 on that September day. Mrs. Irwin was a perfect replacement for Granny and was a good friend. We had many talks and laughs together. No longer did I worry about coming to the dorm, drinking chocolate milk and orange juice from Tarnow Dairy—thanks to Louise Tarnow, a member of that fun-loving class.

Boop and Sue on Affiliation in Marshall

In September, Boop and Sue Murray left for a two-month affiliation at Oaklawn Hospital in Marshall, Michigan. The class of 1951 had the honor of initiating the rural public health affiliation, the first to be established in the State of Michigan. I should mention that this class, in its junior year, requested that Bronson issue student identification cards so they could cash their checks. In their freshmen year, they started a monthly newspaper, called *"51,"* which was published every month.

While in Marshall, Boop and Sue roomed together about four or five blocks from the small hospital at the home of a Mrs. Church. Our letter writing began. We wrote to each other almost every day; we were in love. The week she worked the 3:00–11:00 P.M. shift, I would drive to Marshall, wait for her to get out of work, drive her to Mrs. Church's house and then leave for home. Although it was always after midnight when I arrived home, I felt better knowing she did not have to walk back to Mrs. Church's house alone. Besides, it was only for that one week of her evening shift that I was sleepy while working the next day. The week that she worked the 11:00 P.M. to 7:00 A.M. shift, I came to see her about 9:00 P.M. and left for home around 10:30 P.M., after dropping her off at the hospital.

Expansion of Both School and Hospital

As the new school year began, Miss Mary B. Anderson, R.N., Director of Nurses, announced that Mrs. Helen Weber, R.N., would be the new Assistant Director, Nursing Education, and that Miss Leone Sweet, R.N., would continue as Nursing Arts instructor. Mrs. Weber's appointment would be, as time would prove, to be one of Miss Anderson's most important decisions (since she asked me to work in the dorm).

In October, solicitations began for $991,000 to complete the expansion program. Warren Von Ehren was appointed chairman of the Bronson Methodist Hospital employee campaign for the first of many times that the employees were asked to contribute to Bronson expansions. By December the campaign had raised $1,275,234—*over the top by $284,234*— thanks to the more than 1,000 volunteer workers, industries, businesses, individual citizens, and grants. Bronson employees alone contributed $9,864!

Year-end Holidays

After Boop finished her time at Marshall in November, her folks picked her up and drove her to Sigma Gamma in Mt. Clemens for a two-month pediatric affiliation. I'm sure that her dad was happy that she was 150 miles from Kalamazoo. She roomed with three other classmates. I called her every Sunday night and we wrote letters every day. The week before Thanksgiving, we made arrangements for me to drive up and visit her for

A New Hospital and a New Life

two days. I stayed with an orderly in a building close to the hospital.

I arrived around 3:30 P.M., after getting lost a few times. We went out for dinner and took in a movie before 11:00 P.M. when she had to be back. She had to work the next day, but I was able to have lunch with her before I headed back to Kalamazoo. Although the time was short, we made the most of it.

Before the end of the year, the hospital hired Mrs. Ethel Flower as chief dietician. We no longer had a steady diet of hash and everything creamed. Mrs. Flower came from Chicago, and we now had food that we had only seen at Schensul's Cafeteria. Schensul's up-scale cafeteria was located on Burdick Street, between South and Lovell streets, which later became part of the Kalamazoo Mall. The other big news was that as a result of a vote taken by employees in the sixth floor auditorium, Social Security would be extended to hospital employees beginning January 1, 1951. It was a great way for Bronson employees to celebrate the beginning of the New Year.

For the first three months of 1951, Boop was on affiliation at State Hospital in Kalamazoo. I offered to pick her up at Mount Clemens, but her father vetoed the idea. He chose to travel over snowy roads to pick her up in Kalamazoo, take her to Grand Rapids for a day—then back to State Hospital. Now, after two months in Marshall and two months in Mt. Clemens, we would finally see each other every night, which of course we did. We often double dated with Boop's roommates.

Helping the Students—Again

The exterior structure of the main hospital addition was finished in early January. Workmen concentrated on the fifth floor; hopefully to have 22 private rooms ready in February. As a New Year's gift to the student nurses, Bronson gave them a TV set for the recreation room at Pine Home. As my gift to the student nurses, I offer to set the timer that controls the flood lights in the back of the houses to go off at 10:30 P.M. and not to come back on until 3:00 A.M. (in case the students want to sneak in or out at night).

When a couple of girls told me they would like to get in late, I reset the floodlight clock. The next day, Mrs. Ellis called and said, "Dick, we must have a short in the flood lights—will you check it out?" I tell Mrs. Ellis that I can't find the problem, but if it happens again to call me. She actually called several times, never catching on to what I had done.

Now I will admit to being guilty of a few of the things in the past: placing the girls' pictures of their boyfriends upside down while they were away at class; putting tails on anyone coming into the maintenance shop; starting the grapevine news; and turning on a call light in an empty room, while watching a student answer the call and then have her ask me, "Did you do that?"

I'm Engaged to be Married

On Valentine's Day I picked up Boop at State Hospital to have dinner and stop at my house to visit for a short time with my family. We drove around town, finally stopping by Bronson Park where I told her I had something special for her. Did she suspect what I was about to say, I wonder? Finally, while holding her hand, I declared, "Boop, I love you and would like you to become my wife. I have this diamond ring for you."

With tears in her eyes she kissed me and said, "Yes, I will marry you. Let's go to Pine Home so I can tell the girls." First was Mother Ellis, who hugged both of us. I stayed with Mrs. Ellis while Boop made the rounds to the girls' rooms. After that we left for State Hospital where we said goodnight knowing that this news would spread like wildfire around the hospital. I couldn't wait to tell Floyd and the guys the next day that I was engaged. In fact, I spent the day telling everyone—myself. Jack Tribe thought he would celebrate the good news by having a few cold beers, so while he was away, I washed a couple of patient walls for him. I made the rounds of the dorm telling the class of 1953 that I was engaged. We celebrated with a glass of Tarnow orange juice in the kitchen on the third floor. What great girls they were and are—this class of 1953.

Boop's father, on learning that his daughter had become engaged to me, was very unhappy for two reasons: first, I hadn't gone to college; and second, I was Dutch. I don't know which bothered him the most. As he couldn't change his daughter's mind, he finally accepted the fact that his daughter would be a Vander Molen.

Great Lakes Training Center

With the outbreak of the Korean War, the guys of First Reformed Church wondered if they would be called into service. Already 50 men from our unit had orders to report to the Great Lakes Training Center. Our tour of duty had been extended to 1956. Four of us reported to the fleet in Philadelphia for two weeks training: Bill Brush, the Nelson boys, and myself worked on the Navy mothball fleet. We wondered about guys who fought on these ships in World War II. Strange as it now seems, more than 200 men were called to active duty from our local reserve unit, but none of us from First Reformed Church. We continued to meet every Monday night, and take two-week cruises, until we were discharged in 1956. To this day, we wonder why we were never called up when Dr. Warren Patow, who had been a resident in surgery at Bronson since the fall of 1948, was called to active duty.

Hospital Dedicated and Openings

On April 1, 1951, Hall 5 was renamed *Hall 6*, and opened with 22 private rooms for patients! The rest of the hospital wouldn't be ready until sometime in August. Boop, now back at Bronson, became charge nurse on Hall 6 from 11:00 P.M.–7:30 A.M. Most seniors were also in charge on other floors, which reflected the excellent training they had received.

The Jacob Kindleberger Memorial Chapel

After many years of planning and work by the ladies of the White Cross Guild, a new chapel was built in the

A New Hospital and a New Life

front lobby of the new 1950 building. The Guild, after many years of raising money through bazaars, lawn festivals, etc., finally saw their dream come true as the beautiful, new chapel was completed. Kalamazoo Vegetable Parchment Company gave $50,000 to the chapel fund in honor of its founder, Jacob Kindleberger.

Dedication of the Jacob Kindleberger Chapel was held on May 16th, before an overflow crowd. No one was more proud than the ladies of the White Cross Guild whose years of dedication made the memorial chapel possible. The Bronson student nurses' choir rendered several selections. People were told that the gigantic oak trees would be processed and used in a special way to always be part of the hospital. That was true, but not as they had thought. The lumber was supposed to be sawed into boards and used in various portions of the chapel, including the communion rail, the paneling and a portion of the altar. Everyone thought this actually occurred. "Not so," as I was told by the contractor. The wood was too hard and could not be cut up. He told me this in confidence, and I've not repeated it—until now. "The truth is that I was able to make several gavels from the oak trees which were used at the hospital." That was all of the oak tree wood that was ever used at the hospital's chapel.

The chapel served for 41 years for vesper services, marriages, Good Friday services, meditation, etc. I remember the day that Ward and Ellen Westberg were married in the chapel, and I stood up as Ward's best man.

In June the new heating plant started operating as part of the hospital building program. Floyd is excited about this since he has had much input into this new operation. By the end of July and early August 1951, the new *first floor of the main addition* opened for business. The X-ray, Physical Therapy, and Laboratory were all ready for use. The new Emergency Room would be occupied temporarily by the Surgery Department while the surgical area on the fifth floor of the 1940s building was being remodeled and enlarged. Central Supply on the fifth floor also was in service.

Calling Her Bluff

In July I received a call from Mabel Stell, asking me to come to her office. "Now what did I do?" I ask myself. When I got there she was all smiles.

She said, "Dick, I know tonight is the doctors–nurses dinner dance and you are going to be miserable, aren't you?" Before I said anything, she said, "You come over to my house and I will feed and keep you company so you won't have to think about the doctors tonight." She laughed and I left. The more I thought about it, the more I thought, OK, Mabel, you had your laugh, but tonight I will be over to your house, like it or not.

At 6:15 P.M., I knocked on the door of her home on Burdick Street. Her husband came to the door and said, "Can I help you?"

"Yes," I said, "My name is Dick and Mrs. Stell is expecting me for dinner." He looked puzzled and said that they already had dinner, but "Come on in and I will get Mabel."

When Mabel saw me she said, "Dick, what are you doing here?"

I said, "You invited me for dinner and the evening, remember?"

"Yes, but I was only kidding you," she said.

I replied, "You mean you didn't mean it and now I have missed my dinner at home?" Her husband didn't know what to make of our conversation. "Well," I finally said, "if you are not going to feed me, I'm leaving."

Her husband said, "Why don't you stay for a little while, as long as you are here." So I stayed for about an hour. The next day I told everyone on Hall 6 that Mabel didn't fix dinner for me like she said she would after a special invitation for an evening at her home. I figured I had the last laugh on Mabel.

Boop Graduates

During August and September many things were happening at Bronson. First, the class of '51 was going to graduate on August 24 at the First Methodist Church. Boop was one of the 32 girls graduating, and all of her relatives planned on being there—not only for graduation, but also to meet me. Second, the class of '53 would soon be moving into Pine Home with Mrs. Reusch. Next, Mrs. Ellis had been switched to Cedar Home, much easier for her to handle the quiet class of '52. Then, 62 new students, the class of '54, would be arriving in September. Finally, before graduation, Boop and her three roommates went apartment hunting. I just happened onto a two-bedroom, newly remodeled, upstairs apartment—would you believe?—directly across the street from where I live. The girls moved in and got settled before graduation.

I sit between Boop's sister and grandmother at graduation ceremonies for the class of '51 at the First Methodist Church. I am proud of not only Boop, but for all of her classmates as I hear their names being called. They are pinned by Mary B. Anderson and given their diplomas by Dr. Perdew. I can say, I am proud of every class that I've had the privilege of knowing, and of being able to give them small words of encouragement throughout their three years at Bronson. Boop's graduation gift from her parents is a 10-day trip to Colorado. After graduation, she leaves for Grand Rapids and then on to Colorado. When she returns, she begins the 7:00–3:30 P.M. shift on the pediatric unit. No date has been set, yet, for our wedding.

My good friend of several years, Ruby Smith, had decided to retire. She and I had spent many hours on the third floor of the dorm, visiting and laughing with students from several classes. Another change would soon affect our pocket books—the cafeteria in the 1940 building was about to close and turned into a bakery where Laddie Larva, in later years, made his famous pecan rolls. No longer would we pay fifty cents for a whole meal; instead, each selected item on the menu had its own price.

For Western Michigan College's homecoming parade in 1951, one float Bronson nurses built won first place in the beauty classification, a feat accomplished, with a little help from the Maintenance Department. Our award-winning floats continued for several years, with student nurses riding in uniform on the floats.

New Hospital Solemnly Dedicated

On Sunday, December 9, 1951, the newly completed 121-bed six-story addition to Bronson Methodist Hospital was formally dedicated. I was one of the approximately 450 people who attended the religious dedication rites, held in the beautiful main lobby. The student nurse choir sang several selections. Ralph Tarr, the administrative assistant who replaced Warren Von Ehren, organized the tours conducted during the afternoon.

So, after years of noise, dust, contractors and confusion, we all settled into the new building. Drinking coffee in the snack bar, I pensively watched the cold wind blow snow past the new entrance on Lovell Street. Times were changing once more.

The snack bar proved to be a popular spot for employees and visitors, as well as Upjohn Company employees from across the street. It was open from 9:00 A.M. until 8:00 P.M. Dr. Perdew often came in for a coke and to make sure that only acceptable magazines in good taste were on the shelves for sale. I was a frequent visitor to the snack bar so would often sit next to Dr. Perdew, who didn't stay as long as I did. (That's not hard to believe is it?)

I had been doing the electrical work for the doctors in the three-story medical center and knew most of them by name. Dr. Kilgore took a liking to me and invited me to meet him in the snack bar almost every morning at 7:45 A.M. for coffee and a roll. I barely had time to meet the 7:00–7:30 A.M. crew, and then leave the cafeteria to arrive for my free cup of coffee and roll appointment with Dr. Kilgore at the snack bar. I think he just wanted to talk to someone and that person just happened to be me.

In 1968, Dr. Kilgore, who was both my urologist and my coffee friend for many years, told me he was moving to Prescott, Arizona, where his mother lived. I knew I would really miss him, and have not seen or heard from him since.

When the new cafeteria opened, the service departments' staff could then eat in the dining room with the rest of the employees and student nurses. The doctors could also join us if they chose, and many of them did. Others, however, ate in the two small dining rooms in the back of the main dining area. Jack Tribe and I started going to work at 6:30 A.M. to have breakfast and fun telling the students grapevine news as well as a few jokes before they reported for duty. Many times we were still there when the 7:00–7:30 A.M. students came in for a bite to eat. In time, our crowd grows, so we put together three tables. Everyone wanted to be a part of "The Dick and Jack Storytime."

I still made my light bulb rounds each day. It was kind of neat to see everyone. It no longer bothered me to go into surgery. I stopped now and then to peek into the small round window on the surgery doors and watch the operation going on. That no one ever said, "Dick, please move on," was amazing.

On Saturdays, the doctors held meetings on the seventh floor with coffee and rolls. Jack and I would check in after the meetings were over and help ourselves to the leftovers. While we were drinking coffee on one of these Saturdays, Jack told me he was going to marry Fannie, the long-time telephone operator. She called me several times after they were married, wanting me to look for Jack, so I would make the rounds of the bars until I found him. "Jack," I'd say, "I think it's time to go home."

"After another drink, Dickie Boy," was always his answer.

Boop and Her Roommates

Boop and her three roommates settled nicely into their apartment, and happily received their first paychecks. My taxi service ran constantly since all were on different shifts. Only four or five blocks from the hospital, they walked when I wasn't around (not often).

Would you like a key? From their big sisters, the class of '54 heard to see Dick, the electrician, if they needed anything to be fixed. And they do—especially Al Burns, Barb Funk, Mary Tuck, Joan McNally and Margie Kesselring, to mention a few. At South Home, when I was replacing a blown fuse in the basement, I overhead Judy Stiner tell the girls that she was going to sneak out at night and wanted someone to let her in around 2:00 or 3:00 in the morning. "Judy," I said, "let me give you a key to the house and the girls won't have to set an alarm clock to let you in." Thirty years later at their reunion, I asked Judy if I could have that key back.

B & W . . . How could anyone ever forget Mother Baird and Mrs. Wills—the two women who worked on the first floor of the dorm? This was one of my favorite spots to stop and visit. Of course, this should not surprise anyone. Mother Baird repaired uniforms, and Mrs. Wills sorted uniforms and helped where she was needed.

We Set Our Wedding Date

It's Christmas—Boop and I set May 10, 1952, for our wedding at Boop's church in Grand Rapids. We were excited and wanted to tell everyone. I suggested we tell her folks on Christmas Day, when her family was all home. I did not ask her dad for permission to marry his daughter. Maybe I was afraid of what he might say. I made the big announcement while we were eating dinner. Her dad was a big eater, and I noticed that the announcement didn't seem to bother his appetite. Only later did I learn that he said, "And he didn't even bother to ask me if he could marry my daughter."

Cedar Home

There were two washing machines in the basement of Cedar Home for the girls in both houses to use. They often blew fuses or needed repair. I could have used the side door to enter Cedar Home, but instead chose the back door of Pine Home—especially in the summer when the girls were on the sun deck. I would go through the recreation room, turn on the jukebox and TV before checking out the electrical problems. It seemed like I was always fixing something for the class of '52—a radio that didn't work for Jennie Rasmussen or a desk lamp for Ona Shafer. Maybe it was talking softball with Lou LaRoy or talking with Phyl LeCronier about the time Boop and I double dated with her and Don Curtis, who worked in the lab.

Some of you might wonder if I ever worked—yes, I did, but that's too boring to write about.

Deception

It was late April with the Detroit Tigers playing the White Sox at Briggs Stadium. For this day game, Boop and I, along with my two sisters and their husbands, decided to head for Detroit. First, though, I called Floyd to tell him I was not feeling well, and he told me to stay home. With that taken care of, we headed for Detroit and the start of the game. There were over 35,000 fans that day. Next to me was an empty seat that I hoped would remain empty. With five minutes before game time, I looked down about 15 rows and couldn't believe my eyes. It was Dr. Perdew, and he was headed straight for the empty seat next to me. As the usher dusted off his seat, I stood up and said, "Dr. Perdew, I've been saving this seat for you." He was more surprised to see me, I believe, than I was to see him. He told me he was in Detroit on business and finished at noon and was waiting to catch a train home at 5:00 P.M. To kill time he decided to watch the Tigers game.

The good doctor said, "Dick, you will have to explain the game to me," as he kept apologizing for being there. I didn't tell him about my call to Floyd. My day was ruined. I always yelled throughout ballgames, but this time Dr. Perdew and I ended up only clapping our hands after each good play. When we got home that night, I called Floyd and told him that because I felt better enough to take in a Tiger game, it just so happened I sat next to Dr. Perdew.

The next day I ran into Mary B. and she said, "I hear you and Dr. Perdew saw the Tiger game yesterday."

"Yes," I said, "it was a one in 35,000 chance that we would sit next to each other, but we had a great time." She thought it was funny.

The Wedding

Rehearsal is set for 7:00 P.M. on May 9, 1952, at Burton Heights Methodist Church in Grand Rapids. Boop had been home in Grand Rapids for a couple of days. As I rode up to Grand Rapids with John and Marty Bowers, I thought about how anxious I was to see her. The wedding party included John as my best man; my two brothers Jim and Andy; Boop's sister, Shirley, as her maid of honor; and the bridesmaids were my sister Evelyn and Boop's roommate Ruth Spriggs. My three brothers-in-law served as ushers. Boop's brother Bob was the organist and her brother Roger, the soloist. Maureen, Boop's niece, was the flower girl, while my nephew Phil, was the ring bearer.

Rehearsal went well as the minister guided us through our lines. After the rehearsal party, we all headed home to wait for the big day.

I woke up early on May 10th, knowing it was our wedding day. My sister, Elsie, had breakfast waiting for me and offered some last minute advice. I spent time packing and decided to go to my barber for a shave; I guess I was a little nervous and didn't want to cut my face. There were several errands I needed to attend to, and before I knew it, it was time leave for Grand Rapids.

The Bronson I Knew

I kept asking John, "Do I look OK?" and "How is my hair combed?"

Arriving at the church, we noticed the parking lot was filled with the cars of relatives and friends. Then the minister said, "It's time." I watched with excitement as my beautiful bride came down the aisle with her father. We repeated our vows and the minister finally said, "I now pronounce you man and wife." We kissed, headed down the aisle toward the reception, and later left for a northern Michigan honeymoon. I knew even then how fortunate I was and still am to have Boop as my wife. On our return, we lived at 654 Carr Street, the same apartment that Boop and her friends had lived in the previous year, but was our home for the next three years.

~

7
BOTH THE HOSPITAL AND MY FAMILY GROW IN THE 1950s

Residents and interns were my special friends in the fifties. Two of my favorites were Dr. Herbert and Dr. May. They dropped in often at the maintenance shop, either needing something to be repaired, or just to chat. Dr. Herbert was a great Tiger fan. He would stop in our shop to check on the radio game during the day, when most of the games were played. Dr. May was very proud of the hospital motto, "Where skill and sympathy meet." Another favorite, Dr. King, always joked with Jack and me at the breakfast table. In 1959 Dr. Lubavs arrived at Bronson—he was a real friend to everyone. Many interns and residents have come and gone in my 60 years at Bronson, but the few I have mentioned here are the ones I came to know and appreciate.

The Slippery Tube System

Most of us will never forget the 2-inch pneumatic tube system that went to all nursing stations from a room in Central Supply(CS). When the canister arrived in CS via the tube, the person assigned would send it on to the designated station. Each canister had an identifying number on it, indicating to which unit it needed to be

The Bronson I Knew

sent. Later, this system was replaced with a 4-inch pneumatic system that sent canisters directly to its final destination, without going through CS. Once, when the pharmacy sent a small bottle of glycerin through the tube system it leaked, and then we had the slipperiest tube run in the hospital, from the pharmacy to Hall 6. Never again did it plug up.

Class of 1955

In September we say good-bye to the class of '52 and hello to the class of '55. Mrs. Ketchum, the housemother, greeted this class of 52 girls. They didn't know it yet, and neither did I, but before they became juniors, they will have arranged a big surprise for me.

I could tell that this class was going to be trouble, with a capital T—it began with a flood. On September 19th, Myrt Wise let the tub overflow to make their debut. The halls on the third floor, where she lived, were flooded as well as part of the second floor. The Housekeeping and Maintenance departments were called in after midnight to clean up the mess. What a fun time we had!

With the start of the new year, Barb Gould told me that the Yankees would not only beat the Tigers, but that they would win the pennant. It's hard to believe that this nice class of '53 was so hard on Mrs. Reusch—like putting crackers in her bed, placing x-ray films under her toilet seat or Ex-Lax in her hot chocolate. And—who was it that put icicles in Barb Gould's bed? And I thought I played a lot of tricks.

The baby formula room was located off from the hall near the old cafeteria. Martha, formula room employee, assisted the students in making formula there. As I passed by, I hardly ever resisted putting pictures and jokes on the window. One day, Miss Klute, the dietician saw me, and all the pictures and jokes stopped very suddenly. Miss Klute admonished me, "Don't you have anything better to do?" as she removed my jokes. I felt apologetic to the girls that the baby formula room was going to be very boring from then on. Sorry.

What happened to Dr. Dew? The class of '54 was not without a few tricks of its own. One night a few members of that class were working on the polio ward. Dr. Dew, who had been there for quite awhile, fell asleep on the morgue cart in the hall. Someone covered him with a sheet and wheeled him onto the elevator and sent him down to the basement. I often wonder how many times he rode up and down before he woke up, and what his reaction was.

Personnel Changes

My good friend Jack Tribe, who always said he was "a member of the lost tribe," was diagnosed with tuberculosis in November. He spent the next two years in the Tuberculosis Sanitarium, and the employees took up a collection to buy him a TV set. I really missed Jack. We had had a lot of fun with the jokes we played on so many girls.

Floyd hired Clark Sheldon as a mechanic in early December. He took over the new laundry equipment from me and worked on Saturdays with Ralph Stewart. I liked Clark from the start. Soon we were labeled Mutt and Jeff because he was short and I was tall. In his 60s, Clark often called me "son." Always seen together in the snack bar, we had our coffee breaks at the same time, and he helped take the place of Jack Tribe, while on sick leave.

We're Expecting Our First Child

Oh, have I mentioned that Boop and I were expecting our first child, sometime in August 1953? At breakfast, Marie Jeske, Shirley Martin and Pat Hauke hear the good news first.

With the class of '55 always getting into trouble and calling for my help, I didn't give it much thought when Marie Jeske and Shirley Martin came rushing into the Maintenance Department on a warm summer afternoon. There was a panicked look on their faces as they said, "Dick, come quick—we're really in trouble this time." We ran to the dorm elevator and rode to the third floor and proceeded to room 307, the biggest room in the dorm. As Marie opened the door, the whole class of '55 yelled, "SURPRISE, this is your baby shower." I feebly walked into the room and saw my wife, who was seven months pregnant, sitting in a chair surrounded by many gifts. We were so excited, as we opened presents, ate cake, and drank punch for a few wonderful hours. I have hundreds of warm memories of my working days at Bronson, but I will always remember that special summer afternoon in 1953, when my wife and the class of '55 surrounded me with the surprise baby shower.

At midnight, August 18—Boop's due date—we headed for the hospital. Dr. Birch had been called by Boop, I think because I was too nervous. After three hours of labor, Dr. Birch, all smiles, came out to tell me that we had a red-haired baby girl. Clara Nelson, from the class of '54, was there to assist. I'll never forget the excitement. At 4:30 A.M. I made 10–15 signs saying, "It's a girl," and hung them throughout the hospital. We named her Cheryl Lynn. How thankful we were to have student nurses to baby sit for us in the months and years ahead. During the next year or two, I often brought her to the cafeteria, just to show her off. I was really a proud dad.

Did You See That Fire Hose?

I always drove my own car to pick up electrical supplies from Klose Electric. On this particular day, as I drove down Vine Street and turned north on John Street toward the hospital, I ran over a large hose. For some reason I had not seen it, but felt it as my tires ran over it. About one block from the hospital, I was pulled over by a police officer who inquired, "Didn't you see that fire hose that you ran over?"

"No," I said, "I didn't and if I did and knew it was a fire hose, I would never have run over it."

He said, "Let me see your driver's license." Guess what? It expired two years earlier. So, I received a ticket for the fire hose *and* an expired license. But that's not the bad news.

I told my good friend Clark about what happened. Clark and I had played tricks on everyone for many years, and he took this opportunity to play a trick on me. As luck would have it, I left the next day for a two-week vacation. Several employees knew about my ticket before I left. While I was gone, Clark told the employees and students that because I had argued with the police officer, I had been taken to jail. Can you believe that anyone who knew me would believe such a story? Well, they did. On my return, everyone asked me, "How was jail?" I had a hard time convincing several of them that I was really on vacation. Nice guy, that Clark.

World Series Time

During the World Series, I always ran a pool with the following doctors as my best customers: Drs. Herbert, Jackson, Kilgore, Betz and DePree. With the games being played during the day, I usually found something to do in the recreation room at Pine Home so I could watch the games. Later I watched behind the fireplace in Truesdale Hall, where they had a small room that had a TV. When all World Series games were played at night, my goof-off days ended.

I know I'll miss the class of '53 as they graduate in September; they had a lot of fun while getting an excellent education from the Bronson School of Nursing. Soon afterwards Rev. Robert Trenery joined the Bronson staff as chaplain. Besides his other duties, he would be in charge of religious programs for the student nurses. Mrs. Martha Beatty, social director, continued to invite the students to her home for food and fun.

Bronson School of Nursing—Golden Anniversary

In August of 1954, Bronson School of Nursing celebrated its 50-year anniversary, with special coffee hours including tours and class reunions. It was good to see so many girls who came back for this special event, especially the girls who lived in the dorm when I was "Dick, the Buffer."

Several girls in the class of '54 spent two years at South Home with Mrs. Synwolt, her dog, Freckles, and Josie the maid. Mrs. Synwolt had two major worries. The first was that the girls might let her dog Freckles out, when she wasn't around and Freckles might get pregnant. The second was that I would come to South Home to repair something while she was gone, which I was sure to do. Most of their class spent their time with Mrs. Wotring at Cedar Home and, now on a September night, this class also graduated.

With the arrival of the class of '56 we also said hello to Mrs. Lyons, the latest of housemothers. (Mrs. Synwolt and Mrs. Lyons are sisters). She checked the sign-out book more often than I ever did and wrote and posted her daily notes or poems where they couldn't be missed. She was a woman who came running every time she heard the man bell ring. I sometimes rang it on purpose, and then exited out the front door. I made sure she got her exercise every day.

Boop and I again had a special announcement of our own—we were expecting our second child in late November of 1954. We thought it would be nice to have a boy.

A New Dorm Widely Discussed

As the class of '57 arrived at 419 John Street in September of '54, the need for a nurse's dormitory had been the focus of much talk for several years. Maybe it would happen on their watch? One of the members of this class, Linda Smith, later wrote the words to the School of Nursing's Alma Mater.

Two changes in the hospital administration occurred that fall. Ralph Tarr resigned to begin his new duties at Grand Haven Hospital. Floyd Weddle became the new business manager, and John C. Pratt was appointed assistant superintendent. Mr. Weddle's appointment would mean a lot to the Bronson sports program and the student nurses. He was a "people person," and we celebrated many Christmas parties and talent shows during his years at Bronson.

Both the Hospital and My Family Grow in the 1950s

The class of '55 had heard of Mrs. Reusch's adventures with that shy class of '53. As those students managed a few tricks of their own, Mrs. Reusch stayed on her guard and never told me about the tricks that were played on her, which I found rather strange.

Another redhead was born on November 18—our son. His mother tells me that her grandfather also had red hair. We name our son Craig Alan, and I have my boy. Signs appeared throughout the hospital again, this time announcing, "It's a boy." Now I have two redheads to show off in the cafeteria.

Work on New Accommodations

Bronson Methodist Hospital purchased the Zion Lutheran Church building on Pine Street in May of 1955, to be used for a hospital auditorium and School of Nursing assemblies. Chuck Taylor, a Western Michigan College student who worked in maintenance for several years, helped do several electrical jobs throughout the building. At one time I told him to cut the wiring going to the electric range. When he asked, "Did you pull the fuse?" I assured him, I did. Guess what? Wrong fuse, and he didn't trust me after that.

A big announcement in July—the student nurse dormitory would become a reality. In the fall, a fund drive was launched to build a dorm to house 200 student nurses. The big dorm, Cedar Home, Pine Home and South Home–all would later exist only in memory of good times shared with classmates. For the many girls, as they were a close knit group who lived in these houses, these were fun times.

Graduation Rites

On their last day, members of the class of '55 scurried around the hospital, getting everyone to sign their uniforms. It was always fun signing uniforms, but it was sad to say good-bye to this special class. I always had my yearbook handy so the girls could write in it. As I look back, I can't help but get a tear or two in my eyes when I read what the students wrote. If my smiles helped the students get through training, especially in rough times, then I thank God for allowing me to be part of Bronson and a friend of the student nurses.

Time slips by and we said hello to another class in September 1955. Janet Drake, in the class of '58, broke many light fixtures in her freshman year, but always promised me, "I won't do it again." This class, it seems to me in retrospect, had more tennis players than other classes. It proved to be a good thing as they practiced chasing bats through the dorm with their rackets.

In 1955, some of the residents and interns were Drs. Fry, Zimont, Proos, Wiley, Friend, Kaufman and Camp. Drs. Friend and Kaufman were frequent visitors to the maintenance shop for parts or supplies. I remember watching Dr. Patmos in the parking lot from the window in Pediatrics, with Friend, Kaufman, and probably the girls from the '58 class. After he parked his car for the next ten minutes, he would check every door two or three times to make sure they were all locked before going to his office.

Fixing Problems

The class of '56 had been settled in for several weeks with Mother Lyons. There were exceptions—Joyce Krieger and Bev Richter, who in their little room on the third floor, had many problems with electrical outlets, their desks and you name it. I tried to fix them with Mother Lyons at my side.

While I was repairing a light fixture in a small closet on the second floor of the dorm, Nancy Schott and friends decided to shut the door on me and wouldn't let me out until I say uncle. When I said "Uncle" the door opened and someone snapped my picture. "Hey," I blurted, "I would pose without being locked in a closet!" Well, anyway, the life of the student nurses was not all study and no play.

In their final act of madness, Lou Adams and friends rushed to the maintenance shop and said, "Dick, you are our last hope. We need to get to Paw Paw and back in a hurry—it's an emergency."

"But girls, do you know it's 1:30 P.M. and I work until 4:30 P.M?"

"Please, you are our only hope," they plead once more.

"OK," I said, "but it's against my better judgement." I didn't ask what the emergency was, but we were safely back at 3:00 P.M., and nobody missed me. To this day, I still don't know what the emergency was. I often wondered if it was an emergency or if they just needed something from home.

Plans for New Dorm Continue

The hospital had now purchased a site on the east side of Pine Street, across from North Home, for the new nurse's dormitory. Several houses needed to be razed. In November, a $704,900 campaign was announced to construct a new five-story nurse's dormitory and to remodel the big dorm as a unit for the long-term care of patients. The employees again were asked to be a part of the campaign, which we happily did. The students participated by donating work hours.

The successful campaign for a student nurse's dorm and a chronic patient care unit was a Christmas gift for the hospital and students. The campaign went over the top by $137,185. Of this total $25,000 came from the White Cross Guild, $1,664 from the student nurses, $2,843 from the alumnae, and $10,807 from the employees of Bronson.

Demolition of the seven houses along Pine Street began in January. I watched with the class of '57 from the warmth of Pine Home, with hot chocolate and cookies. See girls, Mrs. Reusch could be nice, even if the cookies weren't homemade! Then, in April 1956 ground was broken for the student nurse dormitory. The total cost of this building will be $1,343,000. Named Truesdale Hall in memory of Mr. and Mrs. George Truesdale, whose bequest amounted to the $225,000 that provided the initial funds for the structure.

Electrical Problems and Prevention

In February, Floyd received a call from Miss Wolters in surgery who reported that the large spotlight in Room I had fallen on a patient. Luckily, no one was hurt and the spotlight, only slightly damaged. A crowd, including Dr. Perdew, Mary B. and a few doctors, had gathered by the time Floyd and I got there. Lyle had already climbed a ladder and found a worn steel pin, which caused the problem. I spent that weekend in surgery, checking the rest of the spotlights and found one in need of repair. From then on, surgery lights were checked routinely every year.

Building a new home . . . The Vander Molens started making plans to build a new home in Parchment, Michigan, that March when Cheri was three years old and her brother Craig, 15 months so they could have a yard to play in. I took a three weeks vacation in May when work actually began on our new house, a three-bedroom ranch. Besides helping with the building, I planned to do all of the electrical work and the painting. Boop and I were excited new homebuilders.

After nearly 13 years as Bronson superintendent, Dr. Perdew had his title changed by the Board of Trustees.

He will now be Dr. Perdew, Administrator. Times continued to change.

On August 27, 1956, Betty and I sat together in the First Methodist Church as the graduation processional began. As Nancy Thomas passed by, I remembered the time I tripped her, as I sometimes did when girls were walking next to me. However, Nancy cured me of this. She turned around and kicked me in the shin, "Thanks, Nancy." When Ginnie Engle followed her down the aisle, I remembered the jokes I told her at the breakfast table—and so it went as the girls passed by. We said farewell to our dear friends in the class of '56.

Truesdale and Vander Molen Construction

The bulldozers and the trucks were busy for weeks, moving earth so the foundation of a new nurse's dorm could be laid. It was the long-time dream of Dr. Perdew and Miss Anderson. We all watched as the concrete was being poured and the walls began going up. This building, which we thought would stand for a hundred years and be a beacon of light for student nurses, was beginning to take shape. On August 27, the cornerstone was laid.

September 1956 was special for several reasons. The 57 girls of the class of '59 would be the last class to live in the big dorm. Although they had a surprise in store for me, which I will tell you about later, Truesdale Hall would be ready in time for the class of '60. After this year, the big dorm, South Home, Cedar Home and Pine Home would no longer be needed for students.

Over in Parchment, I was nearly finished with the painting. We planned to move into our new home on September 25th. With Western students back in class, Mrs. Beatty arranged for a dance to be held in the recreation room. With the jukebox rocking the room and all of the lights and TV set on—the power went out. Mrs. Beatty just happened to have candles in the cupboard, and the dance continued. Mrs. Reusch called me at home to come in and replace the main fuse to the recreation room. The girls said, "Leave the lights off, the candlelight is better." Sorry girls, this was one time I let you down.

September 25 indeed was moving day from the three-year stay in our apartment to our new three-bedroom home in Parchment. My drive to work took a little longer than it used to, especially if I had to wait at a crossing for a train to pass through, but I looked forward to the cafeteria breakfast table waiting for the news of the Tigers and politics. I always got a kick out of Shirley Fetters, from the class of '58, who said my opinions were a little biased.

Who Are We Waiting For?

The bus that took the class of '59 to class to Western each day always waited for one person, before it could leave. Well, now it was no secret; that person was Sheila Robinson. And the reason I know that is, because Mary Roberts told me as I was entering the dorm one day, to go up to the second floor and tell Sheila to stop fixing her hair and get on the bus. "I can't do that to Sheila," I told myself, "let the bus be late." So it was.

Ray Hall used the back of the hospital to bring his patients to the emergency room by November of 1956. Several times Ray traveled alone and when I happened to be near, he asked me to give him a hand. For those of you who remember Ray, he was quite a talker.

As winter set in, most of the class of '57 was on affiliation and the class of '58 looked forward to black-banding. Construction of Truesdale Hall was on schedule, and it was beginning to look like a dorm. Meanwhile, back at the hospital, Miss Huffman was famous for her line, "Girls, you need to function," as they reported for duty. On Peds, Martha Nedervelt, nurse's aide, held a small baby, lovingly talking to it, as only Martha could do.

Pine Auditorium, Capping and the Alma Mater

Three hundred people gather at Pine Street auditorium on February 8, 1957, to witness the 44 young women from the class of '59 receive their caps. Pine Auditorium was the former Zion Lutheran Church. It was at this ceremony that the new School of Nursing Alma Mater was sung for the first time. The next day, the Maintenance Department received a call that the basement of Pine Auditorium was flooded, and we spent a good part of the day carrying buckets of water out of the basement.

The big news in June of 1957 was that student nurses were now allowed to marry. By July the new dorm was nearly finished and dedication only a month away. Mary B. organized a work crew to move all of the chairs, mattresses, stools, etc. from the storage room in the basement of the hospital to the new dorm, via the tunnel. Dr. Perdew, Miss Wantz, Miss Wolters, Mary B., the Maintenance Department and several student nurses worked from 5:00–10:00 P.M. each night, until all equipment was in place. Looking back, it had to be a labor of love.

Dedication of Truesdale Hall

An open house held at Truesdale Hall, August 25, 1957, coincided with its dedication to the service of humanity. Dr. Perdew paid tribute to all who made the nurses' home possible. One day later, 35 nurses from the class of '57 received their pins and diplomas. This was the last class to spend one year in the dorm and two years in the hospital's homes.

A week later—September 1—the day finally arrived when the new and beautiful Truesdale Hall dormitory was ready for students to move in. The class of '58 came from Cedar Home and the class of '59, from the big dorm. Excitement was high, as the move began on a warm summer day. It looked like a small traffic jam on Cedar and Pine streets. Laundry carts were filled with everything from books, clothes, pictures, etc., to small stuffed animals. I remember it well, as I skipped my electrical duties and helped with the move. It was a fun time, as we loaded and unloaded, waited for the one and only elevator, or ran up and down the stairs.

Almost everyone was excited to move into the new dorm, with its large lounge, fireplace, grand piano, television, soft chairs and davenports. Its basement contained many amenities:

- recreation room for dances and parties
- large kitchen to make brownies or fudge
- laundry room
- uniform room led by Mrs. Baird and Mrs. Wills
- sun porch off of the fifth floor, unforgettable by the Maintenance Department
- back yard, with picnic tables and fireplace for cookouts
- mailboxes with the combination locks, located near the elevator
- long tunnel from Truesdale to the hospital where I would, on occasion, turn off the lights when students were half way through and them flip then back on when I heard screams

We welcomed with open arms the class of '60 that had the honor of being the first class to start training at Truesdale Hall.

Housemothers, the big dorm and houses for student nurses are, in the twenty-first century, no longer a part of the School of Nursing, but for those of us who were there, the memories of good and bad times will linger on forever. The title, "Housemother," stopped being used when students occupied Truesdale Hall. Former housemothers were no longer needed and their jobs, eliminated. To those who spent years of training at Bronson, the housemother was a large part of their life, maybe a joy or pain or something in between. I'm certain every housemother will never be forgotten by their charges. The days of fun times and tears are gone. Although we said farewell to the big dorm and all of the student houses, what they meant to us remains in our hearts. What we shared with each other created bonds that link us together for our lifetimes.

My Electrical Work Continued

Back at the hospital, we began working with I-W (conscientious objector) boys, mostly from Indiana. They were required to serve two years before returning to their farms, and they proved to be good workers. Homesickness affected several, but a few stayed after their two years were up and married a student or graduate nurse.

Mrs. Clara Lewis served as Truesdale Hall's house director, and she and I became good friends. Much confusion reigned during the first few weeks, especially at the switchboard, as the electric numbers to the girls' rooms didn't always work. The coin-operated washing machines also had a few kinks in them, so needless to say, much of my time was spent there. Several freshmen whom I met in those early days were: Nancy Peterson, Judy Resh, Marilyn Behnke and Judy Grote, maybe that was because they needed extension cords or had a light fixture that didn't work.

On Hall 2 East, Room 230, a patient for at least a couple of years, was Mrs. Perdew's mother, whom we called Grandma Hale. I became acquainted with Mrs. Perdew as she helped take care of her mother every day. In fact, I believe she was a patient at Bronson for two or three years. I know that the nurses also remember taking care of her. One day the florescent light over her bed burned out and, while I was attempting to change it, the dust flew down and got all over Grandma Hale. I ran to the desk and told the nurses what happened and asked them, "Please come and clean up Mrs. Hale before Mrs. Perdew gets here." Several nurses sprang into action and we all sighed in relief after the dust on grandma and the bed was cleaned up. Where did all that dust come from? The maid hadn't been able to clean the top of the fixture because of the length of time Mrs. Hale had been in the room. The crisis was over—Mrs. Perdew hadn't seen the commotion in Room 230.

Christmas at Truesdale Hall

With the girls' rooms all decorated, a large Christmas tree was placed in front of the beautiful fireplace. Someone at the grand piano accompanied several girls singing carols. I stopped to listen. With all three classes under one roof, it was a blessed Christmas as we celebrated our Savior's birth.

One honor I always enjoyed was crowning the queen at the Christmas formals, which were held in the recreation room at Truesdale Hall. Thank you for asking me, girls, even though I always ended up sitting next to Mary B. for the whole evening. While attending one particular annual Christmas formal, the student nurses asked me to spike the punch, which was in the bowl already on the table along with a variety of finger foods. They were afraid they might get caught with all of the chaperones present. I didn't really want to do it, but after some friendly persuasion, I said I would. They told me where they had hidden the gin or vodka, so when I thought it was safe and almost everyone was dancing, I spiked the punch and quickly moved away from the table. Everything seemed to be going along smoothly, although I did watch to see if anyone tasted the difference.

Don't drink the punch . . . When Dr. Perdew, who never attended the Christmas formal, made an unexpected appearance, those of us "in the know" kept our fingers crossed that he would not get a glass of punch. To our surprise, he raised a cup, and we all got really nervous. Upon tasting the punch, he commented, "That punch is very good. Could I have another glass?" We were happy when he left and did not ask for a third glass. We laughed about it later, but it was the first and last time I ever spiked any punch.

Memories Are All That Are Left

With the beginning of 1958, came the removal of the wooden roof and the fourth floor ceiling of the original hospital (Wesley Hall), and replacement by a steel and concrete roof. "There goes our old attic," I said to myself. This new unit, when finished, would contain 50 beds for the chronically ill. Student nurses would spend one week of duty on this unit and maybe try to figure out where their freshman room was.

In March, while the snow was still on the ground, Mary B. called and asked me to come over to Staff Home, as she had some electrical work for me to do, nothing major and I finished in less than two hours. Two days later, she came into the shop and informed me that I forgot to replace the fuse and everything in their freezer had been ruined. She could see I looked scared and finally after a long pause said, "Don't worry, it's only food." Now do you know why I said Mary B. was my friend?

City League Softball

With spring in the air, we approached Mr. Floyd Weddle, to ask if we might have a Bronson softball team. He checked with Dr. Perdew who approved, so we entered our fast-pitch softball team into the city league. We had the largest cheering section in the league, made up primarily of student nurses. Floyd Rothwell organized a band made up of employees and student nurses that played "Take me out to the ballgame," the only song they knew, every other inning, but we appreciated it. Dr. Perdew appeared to make sure that everyone had a chance to play.

Both the Hospital and My Family Grow in the 1950s

With Bronson's success on the softball field we earned permission to enter a basketball team in the city league. We drew the largest crowds which consisted of student nurses as well as employees. However, our number one fan was Mary B. herself. Miss Wolters and Miss Wantz also attended several games.

Adding a new department . . .In late summer, with more than 600 paid employees, the hospital realized its need for a Personnel Department and Murray Sayre was hired to run it. Since no employee had ever filled out an application form, all were now required to do so.

Here we go again—construction of a three-floor addition to the east wing began in September. The new addition will bring the east wing to the same height as the other wings. The class of '58 won't hear the noise or see the dust since they were graduating, but not so with the class of '61, who enter Truesdale Hall—76 girls in all, which brought the total enrollment to 146.

Who Said I Played Tricks?

On a day in November, Sharon Martin, who had just finished working 11:00 P.M.–7:30 A.M. on OB/Deliveries, was on her way to the boiler room where the placentas were disposed of in the furnace. She stopped and set down the bag of placentas near the stairwell and ran back to the storeroom for a second. As I happened to be there, I took the bag down myself and came back to see what Sharon would do. She said to me, "Dick, did you see a bag here?"

I said, "Yes, I saw Miss Anderson pick up a bag and get on the elevator with it."

"Oh no," she said, "I'm really in trouble now."

"No, Sharon," I said, "I was only kidding—I burned the placenta myself."

"Dick," she said, "that was not funny, but I guess I'll know next time, to take the bag straight to the boiler room."

"I'm sorry Sharon, can I buy you a coke?"

Boop and I have purchased a player piano and who better to help play it than the class of '58? So with plenty to eat, they spent the evening with our family, eating, singing and playing games. We also opened our home to the class of '59 for games, hula-hoops, piano, and more important—food—for a night of fun reminiscent of the days in the big dorm.

In the spring, the hospital purchased the Kalamazoo School Administration Building and Harding School. The administration building was where I went to get my first working permit. Harding School gym will be used by our basketball team for practice and by all students for exercise.

Both the Hospital and My Family Grow in the 1950s

With a Lump in My Throat

It was a day I will never forget. I came to work that warm summer day, not knowing what was in store for me. The day started out as usual. I was at my favorite table in the cafeteria, from 6:45–7:30 A.M., having coffee, talking and listening to the student nurses who were going on or coming off from duty. It was only later in the day that I was to receive the surprise of my life. A couple of seniors came looking for me and asked me to help them in Truesdale Hall. We entered the lobby and the entire class of '59 yelled "SURPRISE." Little did I know or suspect what was about to happen. I looked around the room, everyone smiling. I spotted my wife, Boop, with tears running down her cheeks.

Even now, as I look back, I can never express how I felt as I was presented with a copy of the *White Caps* yearbook. I was stunned and speechless as one of the seniors read the following:

> The senior class proudly dedicates the 1959 *White Caps* to a truly Bronson family...the Vander Molens. Besides providing a home away from home, Dick and Betty have unselfishly helped guide us to our goal. Betty...always capable and dependable, setting a professional example on 3–11. Dick...a sincere friend, always willing to lend a helping hand or an extra word of encouragement. To the Vander Molens

135

> ...Thank you...warmly, simply, sincerely.

I was totally taken by surprise as I fought to keep the tears from running down my cheeks, but I tried my best to thank the class of '59 for this great honor. For the next several weeks, I was on "cloud nine" as hospital employees and doctors congratulated me on this dedication. Even now, I can say that this truly was one of the nicest things that happened to me during all of my working days.

On Thursday, September 3, 1959, sitting in the First Methodist Church, I felt especially proud of this graduating class and the fun times we shared at the breakfast table, the dorm and Truesdale Hall during the past three years. Before saying our good-byes, Betty and I told the girls that we were expecting another baby in late April or early May.

Time to get back to work . . John Kruger, a student at Western Michigan University, had been working with me for several months. He was great to work with, and we had become good friends. Before long, we will have replaced all of the over-bed 2-foot florescent fixtures with a 4-foot fixture. This required several hours of work, plus plastering and painting, before the room could be turned back over to nursing. Meanwhile, John has had his eye on a student nurse—Peggy Mercer, in the class of '60—whom he will marry after graduation.

Floyd is Replaced

In July, Dr. Perdew called all the Maintenance Department employees to the seventh floor auditorium. There was punch, coffee and cookies on the table and we wondered what was going on. Dr. Perdew started out by saying we were gathered to honor Floyd Rothwell for his many years of service as Chief Engineer. He went on to say that hospital policy allowed no department head to continue in that capacity after they reached the age of 65. Floyd turned 65 in June. No outside replacement had been found for him. Later, Mr. Omer Lamothe succeeded Floyd as Chief Engineer and Floyd remained as his assistant.

We were all stunned as he shook Floyd's hand and again thanked him. Dr. Perdew then left, and we hardly knew what to say to Floyd. He took it hard, as did the rest of us. Floyd was my friend—he put his arm around me and said, "It's OK, things will work out."

Time seemed to go fast for me. At that point I had been employed at Bronson for 14 years, and had seen many classes come and go— those years seemed so short. We greeted the class of 1962, knowing that their time too, would go fast, even though they didn't think so during those first several months.

Please let me go . . . As I was walking past the cafeteria, Mary B. was coming toward me. "Dick," she said, "did you happen to see wrestling last night?"

"No," I said.

"Well," she said, "this wrestler from Argentina put a hold on his opponent I'd never seen before. Here, let me show you," she said as she grabbed me.

I should say *crushed me*, and I yelled, "Uncle, please let go." Maybe, I thought, she is getting even with me for that fuse and all that spoiled food. I just hoped no one was watching.

A Backyard Slide

Winter brought a heavy snow, and Craig and I decided to build a saucer slide in our backyard. Once it was done, the student nurses joined the fun, and each year we continued to build it as different classes enjoyed the slide. Several years later, when Craig was a student at Hope College, he wrote the following article for the school paper, *The Hope College Anchor* (1976 March 5):

THE SLIDE

Winter meant one thing when I was growing up. It meant the slide. Before the snow came I would spend long hours peering out the big picture window in the back of the house and watch for the first fluffy flakes.

When the first snow fell I rushed outside and lay flat on my back to see the white flakes meander lazily to earth against the backdrop of the black sky. Rarely did the initial flurry stick, and never did it produce enough snow to cause me to entertain thoughts of beginning the slide. But it was more than enough for me to start envisioning the slide as I lay there.

It would start at the side of the garage, back by where the driveway ended, and zip down the first hill, which was laden with railroad tie steps. At the bottom of the hill stood the big pine. In the summer I killed many an Indian and innumerable Nazis by sneaking down those steps and waiting in ambush behind the wide-based evergreen. But now they were merely incidental. When the slide was finished the steps would be buried for the season and the pine would become just a pine.

At the foot of the hill the ground leveled out for about ten feet and then shot down the second hill, the one covered with honey-suckle. In the middle of the slide stood a once-majestic oak, stunted and scarred by lightening [*sic*]. At the base of the tree was a small opening in the otherwise solidly interwoven honey-suckle which provided me with the best hiding place in the whole yard while playing kick-the-can. Time and again I would curl up in there and wait undiscovered until I became bored, or the itch of real and imaginary bugs crawling all over me forced me to leave.

From my prone position I looked past the base of this hill to the more gentle sloping, open section of the yard. The slide would swing to the east a little there until it got to the skinny maple sapling which marked the top of the final steep downgrade. The sapling was also the point at which the slide swerved back westward so as to achieve the optimum angle from which to hit the wall.

The wall was the hardest part of the slide to conceive of as I lay there. It was also the place, which would require the most time, labor and care. Made of solid snow, the ten foot high wall was placed in front of the road. Its function was to create a corner and send us along the chute parallel to the street, our momentum carrying us about 90 feet into the neighbor's yard. The velocity we achieved as we ripped down the hill dictated the wall's mammoth size.

Both the Hospital and My Family Grow in the 1950s

Anything smaller would be insufficient to stop people from flying over the top and crashing into the road.

Just thinking about the slide made me shiver with excitement, and I knew it would take an eternity for the honeysuckle to be fully covered, that being the sign that it was time to begin construction.

Everyone in the family called it "our slide". But it wasn't. It belonged to my dad and me. We built it; he was the engineer, I was the test pilot. Nary a night went by that we didn't slave over that slide.

There were times when Dad was too tired but I begged and begged until he went out. There were times too when, feeling warm and comfortable, I didn't have any desire to venture out into the cold, barren night. But I was always persuaded. Then I would pull on my long underwear, which always seemed too tight and too short, a flannel shirt, two pairs of pants, huge woolen socks which I tucked my pants into, my old hooded red sweatshirt, my boots and gloves, still wet, stiff, and smelly from a day of school, and my jacket.

Needless to say, this was quite an undertaking and by the time I was finished I felt hot, itchy, and utterly miserable. Inevitably I could not find my black stocking hat, and I went lunking around the house in a frantic search, constantly reminded of the urgency of the matter by the pins and needles which inexplicably found their way into my clothing.

Once outside the cold air revived me and I grabbed four or five saucers, two good ones for riding and the rest cracked, for hauling snow. We worked after dinner mostly, laboring by the warm yellow glow of the street lights and the most distant flood lights which hung above the picture window. The cloth handles on my saucer were frozen and stiff. I fought to get my hands wrapped around them. It would get harder as the night wore on and my fingers became more inflexible.

The beginning was the most tedious time. The slide had to be carved out of the loosely packed snow. Dad would scoop out a little trough and I would hop on my saucer and slide down. Down to the bottom of the first hill, that is. There I came to an abrupt halt, half buried in fluff which flew up and covered my face, the seemingly harmless flakes burning my cheeks. Over and over we repeated this chore. He would dig and pack snow; I would slide down, a little further each time and then climb back up and wait until he signaled me once more.

Climbing up was easy at first. But as the night wore on the top seemed farther and farther away. My boots got heavier, my feet passed from cold to numb to downright painful. The snow would bite my wrists where jacket and gloves did not quite come together. My fingers ached. My ears and nose felt as though they would never be warm again.

Run after run I made, yelling "bump" whenever I hit one. Then Dad would work miracles with the shovel, smoothing them all out. Initially there would be so many that would hit three before I could say anything. Gradually the "bumpbumpbumpbumpbump-bumpbumpbump" rides turned into silent runs. Then we brought out the hose.

Icing down the slide was tricky because the faster it got the higher the wall had to be. When it was too cold for water to flow we reverted to buckets. I would go into the house, fill the bucket, and deliver it to Dad, the theory being that I had more energy and he more expertise in placement.

When the slide was iced it would sometimes go as much as a week without any major repairs. But if we got a fresh snow, higher temperatures, or heavy usage it might last but one night in perfect condition.

Constant reinforcement was also necessary. The strongest and easiest method for doing this was for me to fill a saucer with snow, ice it down, and send it down the hill to Dad who would pack it on the wall or any of the smaller banks. Naturally, since we had a limited number of saucers, I had to run down and retrieve them to keep the process going.

I made the run down the slide so many hundreds of times that the scene is indelibly scratched in my memory. As I was perched at the top, the wind drove

snow into my exposed face like so many
tiny daggers striking again and again at
my raw skin. I was coiled in restless
anticipation, squinting through the night
at Dad, waiting for the signal to go.
When it came I hurtled down the hill
past the snow-covered evergreen and the
menacing brown oak, down toward Dad
who was leaning on the red shovel
which became a fiery blur as I whizzed
by. Going up and around the wall was
probably the most exhilarating part of
the run. Soaring to the peak, zipping
down, and cruising into the neighbor's
yard, I sometimes just sat there, fully
experiencing the wonder. Then I would
rise and start the long trek up the yard
which was ravished by the wall's
demands for snow.

   Though the slide belonged to Dad and
me, it was ultimately mine. He knew it
from behind the wall. I knew it from
intimate contact. I could tell if a bump
was forming, if I rode a bank too high or
cut one too sharply. I could travel down
that slide backward or with my eyes
closed and anticipate what lay ahead,
knowing when to lean left and when to
pull right. When friends used the slide
they experienced the thrilling sensation

of hurtling down the chute. When I went down I experienced the slide.

The honey-suckle is gone now. So too is the old oak. The pine remains but Nazis and Indians have passed there in safety for some years. As I grew bigger, the hill grew smaller though never did it lose its absolute greatness. No longer could I curl up on a saucer; my legs were too long, my damaged knees too inflexible. My younger brother was the test pilot now; I became an engineer. My contact with the slide remained but the intimacy was lost. As I watched Steven hurtle recklessly down the slope, jump up, and start the long climb back, I knew what he felt. Standing there I marveled at Dad, laboring on the wall, and I wondered what memories of younger days danced in his head. What had there been that compelled him to spend night after winter night toiling for reasons his peers would surely fail to understand.

Steve was at the top now, awaiting the signal. Soon the magnitude of the slide would change relative to his own. Then there would be no more test pilots.

Derwin Motyer

Mrs. Gilbert had now joined Mrs. Lewis at Truesdale Hall. It must have been that two women were needed to keep the girls on the right track. Mrs. Weber asked me if I could recommend someone to work as a janitor at Truesdale Hall. I told her Derwin Motyer would be perfect for the job. She hired him, and he stayed until Truesdale Hall closed. He did a great job and the girls really appreciated him.

Who's president? My early morning light bulb rounds were taking twice as long in the expanded hospital because I had several more departments to go through. One example was the new four-room Emergency Department. I always stopped to look at the display case on the wall, with all the foreign objects, which had been taken from patients. What a topic of conversation. I also continued to stop in the snack bar to talk with Mrs. Pidgley and to kid with Drs. DePree, Weadon and Herbert. Because they had coffee together almost every morning, I might ask, "Which one of you is president of the Snack Bar Club this year?" This was at least an annual question.

See a doctor, Dick . . . Did I mention that on my light bulb rounds each morning, I always stopped in Central Supply, located between the first and second floors? I would look to see what message or saying Mrs. Groat had put on her blackboard for the day. I complained to Mrs. Simmons when I had a sore throat, and on several occasions she would take a swab and paint my tonsils with mercresin (which always gagged me), while Mrs. Groat looked on. Finally, I guess she got tired of looking at my throat and told me to see a doctor. I made an appointment with Dr. Fast, and he scheduled me for surgery. He suggested taking out my tonsils using a local anesthetic. Big mistake, as I watched his nurse, Miss Peters, hand him a long needle. I decided to keep my eyes closed—it was terrible. I stayed in the hospital two days. I had lots of visitors and ice cream, and couldn't wait to get back to work.

My happiest years . . . The 1950s were a very special time to be an employee at Bronson, and probably the happiest of my 41 years at the hospital. They were the golden years of hospital employment, as we rallied around our slogan, "Where skill and sympathy meet." Doctors, nurses, employees and volunteers were a dedicated group, knowing we were all doing our job for the benefit of the patients. The average patient stay at Bronson was 7.6 days, and the hospital doors were never locked. Fun times included Dutch Market days in Harding Auditorium with the sale of Olie Bollen (oil or fat balls), baked goods and crafts. Olie Bollen are a Dutch food—deep-fat-fried fritters with raisins or candied fruit, rolled in sugar while they are still hot.

~

The Middle Years

An unauthorized Milham Park picnic, 1950; showing off my navy uniform, 1949; Betty, as she looked when I first met her.

Repairing a hot plate at my workbench, early 1950s.

Mabel Stell.

Dr. Doyle Wilson with me as Santa.

Betty Lou Gosling, R.N., 1951.

May 10, 1952, Mr. and Mrs. Richard Vander Molen.

The Maintenance Department, left to right, Roy VandenBerg, Ralph Stewart, Dick Vander Molen, Floyd Rothwell.

With Nancy Schott, my picture was snapped when the closet door was opened.

My buddy, Jack Tribe (left), and Roy VandenBerg.

Our 1950 crew, back row, Fred, Dick Vander Molen, Paul Lechner, Dennis VanDusen, Ellis Smith; front row, Roy VandenBerg, Ralph Stewart, Dale Duflo.

9

DEATH TAKES TRUSTED LEADERS AND GOOD FRIENDS

In January 1960, private rooms on Halls 3 and 6 were converted to semi-private rooms rather than have patients being placed on the sun porches and in the halls. I spent many, many hours running additional outlets and call systems to accommodate patient load. These rooms were now crowded with two patients per room.

With new calendars hanging at all nursing stations, Clark came up with the idea that he and I should circle October 8 on all of them. So we went all over the hospital, and circled every October 8. Ten months later, when calendars were flipped from September to October, everyone in the hospital was at a loss as to why October 8 was circled and what it meant. Clark said to me, "That's what they get for calling us Mutt and Jeff."

We Say Good-bye to Mrs. Ellis

Although the housemothers had been gone for some four years, I did keep up a correspondence with the Ellis and Reusch sisters; Mrs. Reusch had remained in Kalamazoo, and Mrs. Ellis returned to her home in

Lyons, Michigan. Miss Sweet, who had filled in as housemother for vacations, finally retired and lived in one of the hospital's houses. As for Mrs. Synwolt, Mrs. Lyons, Mrs. Ketchum, Mrs. Ironsides and Mrs. Wotring, it was "so long."

In an earlier year I had gone to Miss Howell's funeral with several members of the class of '47. And, Mrs. Kirk, bless her soul, returned to the big dorm (Wesley Hall), was now remarried to a Mr. Bryant who was a patient on the first floor. "Richard," she said, "come say hello to my husband." He was very sick and lived only a short time, and then Mrs. Kirk was gone again.

Word came to me from Mrs. Reusch that Mrs. Ellis had died on January 31 at the age of 86. On February 3, 1960, I drove my seven–months' pregnant wife, along with Miss Sweet, Mrs. Baird and Mrs. Wills, to the funeral in Lyons, Michigan. It was a bitter, cold day. After the service we went to the cemetery. With the wind blowing and snow on the ground, we all walked over to the gravesite. I didn't know whom to help along the icy pathway. My first duty was to my wife, but Miss Sweet had an asthma attack, and Mrs. Wills and Mrs. Baird were unsteady dodging the tombstones. I was a nervous wreck as I helped Miss Sweet back to the car, and then went back for the others. On the way home, we stopped to see Granny Wright. She was not expecting us, but was thrilled that we had come and welcomed us with open arms. After an hour of reminiscing we said good-bye, knowing that our paths had crossed for the last time.

His Name is Steven

At 8:00 A.M. on May 8, 1960, Betty called me from home, "It's time for me to go to the hospital." We were expecting the arrival of our third child; the other two children were born at night. It was nice to know I wouldn't have to stay up all night this time. At 9:30 A.M., our second boy arrived, and we named this blond-haired child Steven Richard. Once again, signs went up all over the hospital announcing the arrival of our newborn son. And now our family was complete—except for the few cats that we had over the years.

Paging Dr. 33 . . . The hospital had a visual call system for summoning doctors and key employees in case of emergency. Lighted number boards were installed in the major hallways of the hospital, which were controlled by the switchboard operator. If a certain individual were needed, his or her number would light up. Each person had his own number, and numbers were also assigned for emergencies other than summoning individual people, such as when there was a special code call somewhere in the hospital. The code number would light up, and anyone available would call the telephone operator to find out where the emergency was located and then go to that site and provide any help possible.

Several times a week, it was necessary for me to check that all of the lights were working. If a doctor's number was 33 and the bulb on one of the "threes" was burned out, it would show up only as a three and he wouldn't know he was being paged. For years it was my job to do the checking. That all changed when college students began working for us.

The old school administration building on Lovell Street was demolished to make way for a new Bronson Methodist Hospital Visitors parking lot in September of 1960. "Hopefully it won't be used by the downtown shoppers," said Karl Gibson. Unfortunately, it was.

Sports Memories

The class of 1960 was among certain graduating classes that I hated to see leave, after three short years were up. These girls came out to the softball and basketball games, played in the Bronson band, enjoyed the parties at our house, laughed at my jokes at the breakfast table, and helped put on a talent show at Christmas during their junior year. As the School of Nursing class of 1963 entered Truesdale Hall, their members, along with the next four classes, became the cheering section of our sports teams. I often wondered when they found time to study. No problem, since they all graduated.

Bronson's men's basketball team won the league championship as many girls from the class of '63 joined the exciting Wednesday night games. The boys of I-W played an important role in our wins, along with Dr. Roland Springgate, who supplied the team with new uniforms.

Death Takes Trusted Leaders and Good Friends

Eating a hamburger in the shower . . . One day I was in OB/Deliveries talking with Esther Adkins, Sally Reed, Everine Lee and Linda Weiandt. There were no mothers-to-be in the department, so they asked me to run over to Holly's, which was located next to the State Theatre, and pick up some hamburgers. I went out and picked up the hamburgers, and on my return, we all sat in the nurses' locker room and started enjoying those delicious burgers.

Halfway through our meal, Everine got up to answer the telephone and saw Mary B. and Dr. Perdew coming down the hall, heading for OB/Deliveries. She rushed back to tell us and panic set in. I didn't have time to leave, so I hid in the shower room and everyone else made a beeline out of the locker room.

Mary B. and Dr. Perdew explained to Esther that they were looking for ways to expand or remodel parts of the labor and delivery area. While in the shower room, I managed to finish my hamburger and kept wondering what to say if they came into the locker room and found me in the shower. What a dumb predicament to be in. When I heard Mary B. say to Dr. Perdew, "We don't need to do anything in here," I felt a sigh of relief.

After fifteen minutes, they left the department and the girls said, "Dick, you can come out now."

I said, "Hand me a towel, I think I'll take a shower—I've worked up quite a sweat." We all had a good laugh.

Dr. Perdew Dies

When I returned from deer hunting on November 23rd, I heard that Dr. Perdew had been hospitalized for a heart attack. The hospital buzzed with everyone wondering how he was doing. The next day came the news that Dr. Perdew had died. We were all stunned.

Dr. Perdew was a kind, friendly, considerate person. As I sat at his memorial service, my thoughts were of the times that we had cokes together; his congratulations to Boop and me when our children were born; helping him and his wife load their trailer for the annual Methodist Church camp; working the many nights taking furniture to Truesdale Hall; getting called to his office having him tell me in a kind way that I couldn't put up campaign signs for Eisenhower in the hospital; remembering his talk when the war ended; coming out to watch us play ball; his hearty laugh; and his love for Bronson Methodist Hospital. Employees and doctors lost a good friend.

More changes . . . On January 3, 1961, the new Bronson parking lot on Lovell Street opened. Omer Lamothe, now chief engineer, hired two men to collect the money and run the new lot. This was not a parking ramp. John Pratt and Floyd Weddle divided their duties to run the hospital smoothly. We wondered if one of these men would be offered the job of administrator.

Clark Sheldon retired, replaced by Dale Duflo. Virgil Sanford, the night orderly, became the hospital painter. Karl Gibson, the hospital controller, had for the past several years, made his way to our shop each day at 4:00 P.M. I guess he just wanted to feel like one of the boys as we sat around and talked until 4:30 P.M. Maybe he needed to get away from his desk job for awhile.

In May, the breakfast table buzzed with talk that our new administrator would soon be appointed. Dorothy Clark, the cashier, kept asking me if Mr. Pratt would get the job. On June 5, 1961, the Board of Trustees appointed Daniel Finch, as the replacement for Dr. Perdew. It is the beginning of the end for the Methodist influence in hospital affairs—the end of an era for Methodist ministers as administrators of Bronson.

Things Would Never Be The Same

Dr. Perdew often overlooked or didn't know about some of the things we did—like hanging tails on people or throwing a glass of cold water from the seventh floor roof on Jerry, the tech in the lab; turning lights off in the tunnel; loosening the salt and pepper shaker tops; playing pranks on Halloween, etc. We all knew those days were now behind us, as our new administrator took over.

Mrs. Groat, up on the fifth floor Central Supply, had stopped making donuts for her crew. We started paying attention to the length of time that we took for our coffee break. Mary B. was now all-serious—no more wrestling holds. Times had changed and we all felt it.

One day I was in the lobby on my way to the snack bar. I stopped by the information desk to get a glimpse of

The Bronson I Knew

Mr. Finch, who was talking to three other men. When he saw me looking over at him, he said, "Should I know you?"

Without thinking, I said, "No, but it probably would be a good idea if you did." After that remark, I decided not to go to the snack bar. Instead I headed out through the front door and didn't look back.

While no one could measure up to Floyd Rothwell as my boss, I came to respect Omer Lamothe. He rarely took a coffee break, but was always there for me. He and I traveled to many other states, checking on equipment that the hospital considered purchasing.

One day, when Mr. Finch was making the rounds of his department heads, he stopped by Omer's office. Floyd happened to be in the office and offered to show Mr. Finch the boiler plant. Mr. Finch said to Floyd, "No thanks, that's your job to see about the plant. My responsibilities are in administration." When Floyd told me about this I knew that it had hurt him.

Be careful what you write . . . The hospital had purchased new 4-foot fluorescent fixtures to replace all the 2-foot fixtures over the patient beds. As I have mentioned previously, it was my job to replace these in every room, along with my other duties. My thanks go to John Kruger, when he was on summer vacation, and Dale Duflo, for their help. The one thing that I did, and probably John did as well, was to write about politics, people and the Tigers on the walls. The back plate of the fixture covered this. We did this, knowing that chances were good that no one would ever see what we wrote. We were so sure of it, that we signed and dated every fixture. As fate would have it, some 20 years later, all the rooms were remodeled and I was still there. The contractors were getting a kick out of what John and I had written. I was a little embarrassed when reading some of the things that I had written, but also got a kick out of some of the things that I had predicted about politics and the Tigers.

Resignation of Mary B. Anderson

After a little over a month on the job, on July 21, 1961, Mr. Finch had the following announcement, addressed to all supervisors and department heads, posted throughout the hospital:

> ***Subject:*** Resignation of Director of Nursing
> Announcement is being made of the resignation of Mary B. Anderson, R.N., as Director of Nursing of this hospital effective immediately. No new director can be named at this time. However, until such time as a successor to Miss Anderson can be found, all questions related to the office of the Director of Nursing will be referred to Miss Marie Wantz, R.N., Associate Director of Nursing for Nursing Service, or Mrs. Helen Weber, R.N. Associate Director

> Nursing Education, as the case may indicate.
>
> Daniel N. Finch
> Administrator

This notice was posted so everyone who came to work that morning saw it. It was probably met with mixed feelings from the nursing personnel. For me, Miss Anderson had been a friend. Known only to a few people, Mary B. had given large sums of money to the hospital. Her heart and soul was for and about her love of Bronson, Truesdale Hall and nursing in general. Miss Anderson had no trouble finding another job, as she was appointed Director of Nursing at a hospital in Des Moines, Iowa.

During her years in Des Moines, she traveled to Fremont, Michigan, each fall to spend time with Dena Wolters and Marie Wantz. Mary B. would always stop at our house for dinner, smoke several cigarettes and reminisce about those special days in the 40s and 50s. It was at our house that she told me about her firing and I could still see the hurt in her eyes.

As the special class of 1961 received their pins at graduation, Miss Anderson was absent. This marked the first time in many years that she had not pinned a class at graduation, as Mr. Finch handed out the diplomas. This class had more girls at the softball and basketball games than any other class. So long my friends, and God bless.

Another Resignation

Mr. Weddle told me it was only a matter of time before he left. One of his duties was to oversee the Maintenance Department, housekeeping and laundry. Mr. Weddle was our coach at first base and never missed a game or practice. I was thankful we won our first trophy in softball before he left in the fall. It was a tribute to him for all that he had done for our team. Mr. Weddle accepted a job as the administrator of Allegan Hospital.

In 2003, Mr. Weddle stopped at Bronson for a chat with Frank Sardone, and asked about me. I was able to make contact with him at his home in Muskegon. Betty and I made arrangements to have lunch with him in Grand Rapids, to renew old friendships. After a couple of hours of talking about his years at Bronson, the ball team, Dr. Perdew's death, and the events of those months before Mr. Finch was hired, we said good-bye to our dear friend. We have only kept in touch by phone since that time.

More Housing Changes

South, Cedar and Pine homes became the homes of resident physicians, and I found myself doing the electrical work for the doctors and their wives. Things seemed strange, because the recreation room was now empty, and no TV set or jukebox were around—only memories of those days, now so long ago. Anderson Hall on John Street, named for Miss Anderson, and home for the practical nurses saw a change of residents. Dr.

Dvorak's family lived there and the sign, "Anderson Hall" had been removed.

Houses along John, Walnut, Jasper, Kook, Pine and Vine streets were purchased, one at a time, over several years. I always enjoyed going through these empty houses, checking out the attics and looking through things that were left behind. In the basement of one of the houses on Pine Street was a fruit cellar with many bottles of dandelion wine. When the contractor began to demolish the house, the men located the wine. It must have been pretty potent stuff because we didn't see the men for a week.

Mr. Pratt's Last Official Function

At the Employee Service Award banquet held in Truesdale Hall's recreation room in November, Mr. Pratt presided and presented pins to the award winners. It was the year that I received my 15-year pin and I told him, "Thank you, Mr. Pratt. I'm glad it was you who gave me this award." Mr. Pratt left Bronson in December and became president of a large hospital in Louisville, Kentucky. He left Bronson a very bitter person, and has refused all correspondence with me. I feel badly about this because I considered him a good friend.

Ward Westberg was hired over at the boiler plant. I knew Ward from my Navy Reserve days. Friends then, we have remained close throughout our retirement years. With Mr. Pratt, Mr. Weddle and Miss Anderson gone, Mr. Finch appointed Stuart A. Wesbury, Jr. as the new assistant administrator and Miss Virginia McPhail, R.N., a 1948 Bronson graduate, as director of nurses.

Class of 1964

Marjorie Gilbert and Louise Dillon as residence directors, greeted the class of '64 at Truesdale Hall. Helen Weber directed nursing education and Hazel Latondress, the house supervisor, took charge of whatever needed to be done at the hospital. This class of '64 dedicated their yearbook to a very special person—Mrs. Louise Brown, who as secretary to Mrs. Weber, had helped so many students over the years.

How could I have been so busy? At Christmas time in 1961, I received the following note in a Christmas card from Floyd, "Dick: We don't see each other very often anymore and the old times may be gone, but I want you to know I still appreciate your *good* friendship—Floyd." I was touched by that message and have kept it all these years.

"Where have I let my friend down, who was so good to me," I kept asking myself. While Floyd was my boss and his new office was located in the basement near the boiler room, he always made his way to our shop after lunch and spent time with us before returning to his office. It's true, times have changed but I should have found time to have coffee with him. I owed him so much. Times do change, but not friendships, and this card was a wake-up call. I decided from then on I'd make it a point to call Floyd for coffee so we could talk about those days when he was my mentor, and so I did.

Finding a New Doctor

Dr. Harold DePree, who had been our family doctor for many years, was appointed by Daniel Finch to be director of medical education. He began his new duties on June 1, 1962. I didn't know how this would affect his "snack bar club" coffee hour, but Boop and I had our medical records transferred to Dr. Doyle Wilson.

Mr. Finch sent a letter to all employees in the spring, telling us how important we were as members of the Bronson family. With that in mind, he informed us that new personnel policies pertaining to vacation, holiday, leave of absence and sick pay have been improved. Also, sick time would be increased from five to eight days per year. That sounded pretty good to me.

School of Nursing Graduation

In late summer, 37 girls from the class of '62 received their diplomas and pins at the First Methodist Church. A member of this class was Jackie Clark, who became the director of nursing education following Mrs. Weber's retirement.

December 31, 1962, saw Miss Wolters and Miss Wantz retire from Bronson Methodist Hospital. Miss Wolters, was the Operating Room supervisor, and Miss Wantz, now assistant director of nursing, was previously the Obstetrics supervisor for many years. I knew that ever since Miss Anderson's firing, these two looked forward to the day when they could retire to Fremont, Michigan. During their years in Fremont, many a Bronson graduate stopped in to see them. Betty and I called on them a year after their retirement, and Miss Wantz was still upset about her good friend Mary B. getting fired. In September of 1964, Miss Wantz died of a heart condition. Several years later Miss Wolters also died.

Changes in Dietary . . . In 1963, Mr. Finch announced big changes in the Dietary Department. No longer was Miss Helen Klute the department head because George Alexander and Gus Lecos from Szabo Company had signed a contract to run it. Food we never knew existed now appeared in the cafeteria. Miss Klute, no longer in charge of dietary employees, had become the Executive Therapeutic Dietician. We in the maintenance shop formed a great relationship with Gus. We helped him with his ice carving, and he saw to it that a watermelon appeared in our refrigerator every so often.

First *Catalyst* Published

The first employee newspaper, which initially was unnamed, was published in June of 1963, with the editorial staff composed of Gus Lecos, Helen Klute, Mabel Meyle, Ralph Meyer and Murray Sayre. How could this newspaper fail with such reporters as Jr. Ashby, Dorothy Clark, Mary Mason and me? The newspaper would be published six times a year.

An employee contest was held to name the newspaper. The winner was Linda Cutright, a senior student nurse, whose winning entry was, *The Catalyst*. Those of us who could find time to get away, assembled it in Harding Auditorium, page by page. At times, Jr. Ashby and I got to goofing off and Mabel Meyle said, "Stop, or I'll report you." With her voice of authority, that's all that we needed to stop.

Play ball!!! On June 8, I arranged a bus trip to Detroit to watch the Tigers play the Yankees in a night game. Forty-two employees left Bronson at 4:00 P.M. for Tiger Stadium. On board were the two MacDougal sisters from Scotland. They knew nothing about baseball, so I made sure that they didn't sit next to me. I wanted to yell, not explain the game. It was a great game—the Tigers won 8 to 4.

Everyone had been told exactly where the bus was parked before we entered Tiger Stadium, so when the game ended we tried to leave for the bus as a group. I counted heads when I thought that everyone was back, but came up with two short—the MacDougals. We waited for a half-hour. Then I said to Ward Westberg, "You go around Tiger Stadium to the right and I will go around to the left and hopefully when we meet, one of us will have found them." No luck. We came back empty handed. This time we walked back to the bus together feeling much safer in numbers.

After another 30 minutes of waiting and trying to figure out what to do, the MacDougals finally showed up, not giving a clue as to where they had been. We were all thankful that they were back safely, but no one ever found out what happened while we waited for them.

There go our fans . . . At the graduation of the class of '63, we said good-bye to a large group of our sports program supporters. Bronson was the team with the most wins in the city league in the 1960s. Our men's fast-pitch softball teams won six league championships with two undefeated teams. In basketball we won four league championships. Many thanks to our players, the hospital band, the nurses and employees.

Tragedy and The Camera Crew

November 22, 1963 . . . I knew when I came to work that this was going to be a long and tiring day. What I didn't know about, was the tragedy that would take place shortly after lunch. I was working on the OB fourth floor on the day that President Kennedy was shot and killed. A camera crew from Hollywood, California, was filming a special surgery case in OR. At that time the OR was located on the fifth floor.

We in the Maintenance Department had, for several months, made plans and preparations for the filming. A special platform had to be built for the surgery in Room #4. Additional electrical lines had to be installed from the panel on the fourth floor for the camera crew's equipment. Wiring was run from the panel on the fourth floor up the stairwell, across the hall on the fifth floor to Room #4 in OR   (Got the picture?) It was only natural that I found myself glued to the panel on OB to make sure the wiring did not come loose.

Shortly after 1:00 P.M. a nurse passed by. She was carrying a baby to the mother, and told me that the president of the United States had been shot in Dallas. She had heard it on the TV located in the fathers' room, near the main nurses' station. Unable to leave the fuse panel, I was beside myself. Minutes seemed like hours before someone would come by with additional news. Finally, I decided I couldn't take it any longer and left the fuse panel and ran to the fathers' room to hear Walter Cronkite tell that President Kennedy had died. At that moment in time, the tragic news was more important to me than the filming going on in surgery. After a short time, I returned to the fuse panel. The camera crew finished filming at 3:45 P.M.

I will never forget the next hour at the hospital. Throughout the hospital, people were crying. There was disbelief that this could happen. Everyone seemed in shock. It was a scene that would be repeated over again five years later, as both Bobby Kennedy and Martin Luther King, Jr., were assassinated in 1968.

In December, Chaplain Robert Trenery announced his resignation from Bronson Methodist Hospital, effective June 14, 1964. It caught all of us by surprise as the good chaplain let it be known that he would probably retire from Bronson and a job he really enjoyed.

A Different Christmas

Mr. Finch told the Christmas Committee, of which I was a member, that the employees would not have a Christmas party this year. Other members of the committee included its Chairman, Mr. Alexander, and Mr. Lecos, Mrs. Pidgley, Floyd Rothwell, Miss Mason and Mrs. Gilbert. Mr. Finch had decided that the children from the clinic would be our guests and that we would serve them a Christmas dinner at Harding Auditorium. End of discussion. And so, it was the first time ever that there was no employee Christmas party. We all did help in making the children feel welcome, with food and gifts. We were one of several organizations that saw to it, that all the children had a wonderful Christmas, but the next year, the employees once again enjoyed their annual Christmas party.

Building Expansion

If my memory serves me correctly, 1964 saw no major building taking place at Bronson, surprising as it may seem. This does not suggest that no major building project was being planned—it was. In 1964, employees were again asked to contribute to the Building Fund and over $58,000 was collected.

As the hospital continued to expand, so did all of the service departments. Omer Lamothe, Chief Engineer, divided the Engineering Department into two sections: Maintenance and Plant Operations. Floyd Rothwell served as Fire Marshall for the hospital and conducted fire safety classes. The Engineering Department then consisted of 25 men who worked in the areas of mechanics, carpentry, electrical, painting, and the parking lot, plus firemen and yardmen. Ward Westberg and Paul Lechner were appointed supervisors. I was named assistant supervisor of the Maintenance Department, but continued to do the electrical work.

Give me a break! The hospital business office, at that time, was located off the main lobby in a large room. It seemed that every other month a ballast in one of the florescent fixtures in the business office would burn out, putting half of the room in darkness. These fixtures were a pain in the neck to work on and so was the replacement of the ballasts. The women always asked me, "How long is it going to take you to fix the lights?"

I would reply, "Maybe an hour if I'm lucky." We would repeat this conversation every time a ballast burned out. Oh, for those days in the dorm, when all that I had to do was to change a light bulb!

The hospital owned several homes along Jasper Street that were used to house residents and interns. These older homes also required electrical or carpentry work from time to time. It was a nice walk from our shop on John Street to Jasper Street, especially during the summer. It was only a matter of time before these houses would come down to make room for a new power plant.

Final Farewells to Two Good Guys

One day in July, while having coffee in the snack bar, Floyd told me that he was having chest pains. I asked him if he had seen a doctor about it. He said no, that maybe it was something he ate. He said that since his wife had died the year before, he was not only lonely, but that his appetite was gone. He began coming over to the shop more often again, talking to Roy, Ralph and me. It seemed like old times.

In early September Floyd missed several days of work. When he came back he told me his chest pains were getting worse, and he had made an appointment to see a doctor. He was admitted to the hospital around the 19th of September. There was a "no visitors" sign posted on his door. Floyd's son, Bob, was in the hallway when I came by. He said I could go in see Floyd for a few minutes. "Floyd, it's Dick," I said as I held his hand. He looked up, didn't talk, but just squeezed my hand. As I left, I knew my friend was very sick.

On September 29, Floyd died. I just wanted to be alone, so I rode the elevator to the seventh floor, went out on the roof and cried. I had lost my friend. If it hadn't been for Floyd, I would never have had the opportunity to work at Bronson Methodist Hospital. He and I both had something in common—our love for Bronson. I always felt there was a certain bond between us, like a father and son. At his funeral I said my farewell to this special person and the role he played in my life.

At the Employee Service Award program, held in Harding Auditorium in November, Lyle Nottingham received his 30-year award from Daniel Finch. Lyle was the orderly in the operating room. He was always there for the student nurses. Then there was Lyle's closet, where I have to believe it was the doctors who put up the pictures of Marilyn Monroe, etc. I checked it out, from time to time, to see what new pictures might appear. I'm thankful to Lyle for his helping hand when I had to repair equipment in surgery. Ten years later, Lyle received his 40–year award. It was at the time that the new surgery unit opened. After receiving his award, this time Lyle, in his quiet way, just simply walked out the door and never looked back.

Lyle Nottingham passed away on September 14, 1991. He will be remembered by many of us as a friend and to many a student nurse as a sweetheart. I recall many mornings at the breakfast table in the cafeteria, listening to the student nurses tell how Lyle had helped them and had come to their rescue. He did everything from moving patients from the various units to surgery, to mopping the surgery floors, waiting on doctors and fixing equipment. Miss Wolters often said, "I don't know what I would do without Lyle," and I know that many of us felt the same way. We all have special memories of him from our days in surgery. He was truly one of the good guys.

~

10
PEOPLE, EXPANSION, PROMOTION

Work began in May 1965, on the first phase of Bronson's newest expansion program, ground breaking for a new boiler plant to be located east of old Harding School and north of Truesdale Hall. Other phases would include the addition of the seventh and eighth floors of the hospital. A late decision to add ninth and tenth floors to the hospital was rationalized for storage until they would be needed for patient rooms. Ward Westberg and I were frequent inspectors with long-term interests, as construction of the power plant took shape.

Maintenance Department Supervisor

In June, with changes in coding maintenance card systems and pressure for additional work to be done, Paul Lechner wanted out of management, and I was appointed supervisor of the Maintenance Department. I received permission to hire four more employees in the next two months. This was a new experience for me, interviewing people for jobs, but one I enjoyed. Over the years I hired several students from Western Michigan University for part-time employment for work on weekends, after school and during summer vacations. Not only did we help these students with a paycheck, but they also gave us a little cushion in our work schedule. They proved to be good workers. The best was John Kruger who did many special projects with me. He was dependable and could handle any emergency. I really missed John when he left for Greeley, Colorado. John and I have kept in touch through the years.

At the service award dinner on November 3, 1965, five employees who would retire at the end of the year were recognized:

- Karl Gibson, controller, was special friend to us in the maintenance shop. Later I did some wiring at his home on Miles Avenue. I think he was more interested in what was happening at Bronson than having me do some electrical work;

- Roy VandenBerg, carpenter, my partner on Saturdays and holidays. Although he was a Democrat, we had many good talks. Roy could fix about anything and I learned much from him;

- Hilda Pidgley, manager of the snack bar, a dear for letting Dr. Kilgore and me have coffee and a roll in the early morning before the snack bar was open. She was from England, and told me what World War II was like there. It was hard to imagine what difficulties they survived.

- Jerry Heydenberk, chief inhalation therapist. I enjoyed Jerry and his sense of humor. He spent time in our shop while we fixed things for his department. He was my 500-card partner during

our wintertime lunch breaks and in the summer he was my horseshoes partner.
- Harvey Meyers, laundry manager. Harvey ran a tight ship in the laundry—all work and no visiting. In his last year he mellowed quite a bit and would occasionally enjoy a coke with me.

All five played important roles in my days at Bronson. They were long-term employees whom everyone would miss, but I missed Roy VandenBerg the most.

Building and Personnel Changes

Mr. Stuart Wesbury, after serving as assistant administrator of Bronson Methodist Hospital for four years, announced his resignation in January of 1966. He was leaving Bronson to assume a hospital position in Florida. Jack Schwem replaced him. I remember getting Mr. Wesbury interested in state politics, but Mr. Finch didn't think it was a good idea, and the boss had the last word.

The following month, the medical conference room on the third floor of the Harding building opened as a place where doctors met on Saturdays, from 8:00–9:30 A.M. Coffee, rolls, and pastries were always available at these meetings. If the interns and residents didn't take the leftovers home, Ward and I ate them. Department head meetings were also held in this conference room.

During 1966, new people filled several key positions. In March, Harold Slates was hired as the new laundry manager; Rick Geer began his duties as personnel director in May; and Mike Lampos began his duties in July, as assistant food director, reporting to Gus Lecos. Having begun their lives as new members of the Bronson family, in time, all three of these men would need my services as supervisor of the maintenance shop. Things they would need included equipment repair, remodeling, painting, etc.—all became the focus of new relationships for me.

Donny Fee

When my son, Steve, was seven years old, I received a call from school that he was very sick. So I left work, picked him up and took him to the emergency room. The doctors, after hours of testing determined that he had a gall bladder attack and scheduled him for surgery. He was a patient for the next week, in a large room in Peds, with several other boys. I visited Steve's room several times a day, and became acquainted with a little boy named Donny Fee who was in the bed next to Steve.

Donny told me this was his second time back in the hospital. He also told me about his schoolteacher and his brothers and sisters. He was a nice little boy whom I felt very close to. When the day came for Steve to go home, I said to Donny and his mother, "I will be back to see you every day until you go home too." Donny was there another week and I saw him several times a day.

One day Donny said, "Dick, I'm going home tomorrow and maybe back to school." As he left with his mother the next day, I said, "Good-bye, my little friend. I'm going to miss you. Have fun at home and school."

It was three or four months later that I received a call in the shop from Peds telling me that someone wanted to see me. It was my little friend, Donny. "Hi, Dick," he said from his private room, his voice was weak and his stomach bloated. "I got to go back to school and I like my teacher," he said as his eyes lit up.

"Is this your Bible, Donny," I asked.

"Yes," he said, "and Jesus is my friend."

I said, "He's my friend too." When the nurse came in I told Donny I would be back to see him and left to go back to work. I saw Donny several times a day after that. I brought him packages of baseball cards, and he was excited if a picture of a Detroit Tiger was in them. His mother told me that Donny was given only a short time to live, which I could tell. His stomach looked the size of a basketball. "Dick," he told me one day, "next week is my birthday and my mother is bringing me a cake. You can have a piece."

"That's great," I said, "and what do you wish for your birthday?"

"I don't know," was his answer, and after he thought for a minute, he said, "I've never had a two-wheel bicycle."

I asked, "If you got one, what color would you like?"

"Blue," he said without hesitation. When I left his room I knew that Donny was going to get that blue two-wheel bicycle. I first talked to the nurses and then to the guys in the shop. The day of Donny's birthday party, I wheeled in his blue bicycle. He was so excited, and despite the fact that he was so sick, he wanted to get out of bed and sit on it. The nurses helped him, and he sat on his new bicycle and said, "I thought I would never have a bicycle."

He returned to his bed, and we had a piece of cake. With tears in our eyes, we sang "Happy Birthday" to him. Each day that I came to see Donny, his bike was next to his bed—he was so proud of it. Then, each day Donny told me he was going to heaven to see Jesus. His pastor was there every day, and would read and pray with Donny. Many days when I went into his room, his Bible was in his bed with him.

Then the day came when I went up to Peds and saw an empty room. Donny had died during the night, with his mother and dad at his side. My comfort was that he was with Jesus, whom he knew loved him very much. After the funeral, his mother told me that Donny wanted his brothers and sisters to ride his bike. It's been over 35 years since Donny was taken to heaven, but I often think of my little friend.

People, Expansion, Promotion

Laundry Fire

I was talking to Harold Slates on the phone one day in June, suddenly someone yelled, "We have a fire in the laundry." Shouting at the maintenance guys to go to the laundry room because there was a fire, Harold and I each grabbed a fire extinguisher and also start running to the laundry. The ironer was on fire, but we succeeded in putting it out. Thirteen laundry employees received an unforeseen holiday (with pay, I hope) until repairs were made.

In August, the Laboratory Department moved just down the hall to its new quarters, between the main hospital and the Harding building. Although the new outlay consisted of 23 new rooms and the employees were happy to have more elbow room, they didn't realize then that they would be expanding again, at least twice, in the years ahead. Each of these expansions involved the Maintenance Department in one way or another.

Mr. Finch announced in December, that plans had been made for a new laundry. It would be underground between the Harding building and Truesdale Hall. Work began with the pouring of several new foundations. Then, almost as soon as construction started, it stopped. Much to the dismay of Harold Slates, his new facility was never built. In the years ahead, Kenny Powell repaired the old laundry equipment and kept it in running condition.

Department heads . . . Before the end of the year, Ward Westberg and I were promoted to department heads. Our

181

boss, Omer Lamothe, introduced us at the department head meeting. This part of my journey as Maintenance Department head would continue until February 1, 1986, the day I retired at the age of 56. During the previous years when I was the hospital electrician, however, I became indebted to Harold Viel and Gordon Zwart, the electrical contractors, who always gave me a helpful hand and words of advice. The same thing can be said for Ben Korendyke, the superintendent from Miller-Davis, and for Jerry Pinkster and John Titus from the architect's office. For these men, I will be eternally grateful.

The Big Snow

Who of us at Bronson on January 26, 1967, will ever forget the big snowstorm? Many of us were stranded at the hospital for days. Housekeeping and maintenance prepared mattresses and bedding in Harding gymnasium and auditorium for the use of employees and visitors. Dale Duflo, several other maintenance guys and I slept in the maintenance shop on whatever we could find that looked comfortable. I don't remember that any of us got much sleep, but the next day we all pitched in wherever we were needed. Rick Geer helped with the cooking, some of us worked in the laundry or housekeeping. The student nurses helped out on the floors. Daniel Finch said it all, "The snowstorm brought out the good in people." I was finally able to get home after being stranded at the hospital for three days.

In the spring, employee badges were initiated. All employees were to wear them when on duty. Years later, our picture appeared on our badge; mine looked worse than the one on my driver's license.

My boss resigns . . . Omer Lamothe, chief engineer, who had been my boss for several years, informed Ward and me, that he would be leaving Bronson in July for a job in Louisville, Kentucky. Omer had been involved with so much of the hospital construction—seventh and eighth floors, the power plant and the laboratory. It was not news I wanted to hear. Omer had been a good boss and I learned much from him. Late in the day he called me to his office and said, "Dick, I have permission to send you to the School of Public Health at the University of Minnesota, for a six-week course in hospital engineering. It's a course that I have always wanted you to attend—it will be a great opportunity for you. I hope you will go."

Without hesitation I said, "Yes."

"Good," he said, "I knew you would, and we already have you registered." Omer would not leave Bronson for another month, so I made sure I spent as much time with him as possible. Before I left for Minnesota, I made arrangements for the guys in the shop to give Omer a big farewell party.

University of Minnesota

I arrived at the University of Minnesota on Saturday, July 15, and was assigned a room in Centennial Hall. The following Monday I attended my first class with 33 other guys, all involved with hospitals throughout the country, and on Friday, July 22, I called Bronson's maintenance shop. It was Omer's last day. I wanted to hear how the party was going and to say a final farewell to Omer.

The first two weeks of school went by fast, as we were in class from 8:30 A.M.–3:30 P.M. every day. I wrote and called home several times a week. On several occasions I received a call from Bill Brush, who was working at the Upjohn Company. During the first week of August, I received a call from Ward Westberg, who asked, "Dick, what do you think about me applying for Omer's job?"

I replied, "Ward, go for it. I would like nothing better than to have you for my boss."

"OK," he said, "I'll see W.E. Johnson [who was our department head], and tell him I'm interested in Omer's job."

I didn't hear anything for a week, but when I finally received a call, it was from W.E. Johnson. He said, "Dick, what do you think about Ward taking over Omer's position?" I told him I thought it would be a good choice as Ward was familiar with the buildings and all of the construction that was going on. "OK," he said, "if you're comfortable with it that's what I needed to know."

Ward promoted . . . Therefore, on August 30th, Daniel Finch announced the promotion of Ward Westberg from supervisor of Plant Operations to Plant Superintendent, a newly created position to replace the position of hospital engineer. Then Frank Elley was promoted to Ward's old position, and Peter Froyd joined Bronson on September 11, as assistant administrator. Many years later, I reported to Mr. Froyd.

"Well, I'm back," I told the guys in the maintenance shop. "I hope you missed me. I know my family did." I congratulated Ward in his office, then we celebrated with a milk shake in the snack bar.

Open House

A planning committee, of which I was a member, organized an open house for the power plant and seventh and eighth floors on October 27–29. As anticipated, thousands of people attended. Ward and I both said it would have been nice if Omer could have been there to show off the power plant.

Bronson trustees had announced plans for a three million-dollar expansion program for the pediatric–adolescent building earlier in the year. So on Friday, December 22, workmen with bulldozers began tearing down homes on the south side of Cedar Street, between John and Pine streets. Many readers will remember Dr. Sherman Andrews' office building which was one of the first to go. Next was Anderson Hall, followed by Cedar and Pine homes, in the spring. Cedar Street as we knew it would be closed and relocated one block south.

Mother Baird retires . . . I thought it important that all student nurses knew that Mother Baird was retiring at the end of 1967. Mrs. Baird had been employed at Bronson for thirty-seven and a half years, most of them as a seamstress. She was known as Mother Baird to most of the students whose uniforms she always sewed and mended so neatly. And to me she was a dear friend.

The Snyders

Some of the people who worked at Bronson will never be forgotten. For me, they include the Snyder brothers. They lived with their folks on a 30-acre farm one mile north of D Avenue, in a home with no electricity. Harold was the oldest and worked in surgery, as an orderly. He was proud of his perfect attendance record for over 20 years. Caspert, a few years younger, was a janitor in the Housekeeping Department. What's really remarkable about these two is that during the great snowstorm of 1967, they walked ten miles to work through all of that snow, arriving only a few minutes late. Can you believe that? After their shift, they walked back home again.

Harold never drove a car and always rode with Caspert. Before working at Bronson Methodist Hospital, Caspert had been employed at the Harris Hotel. After leaving the Harris, he continued parking his car there, and then walked five blocks to Bronson to work. This he did during his entire employment at Bronson.

Caspert liked to talk with me. Some of what I remember concerned his car and about when he and Harold took a big, one-day vacation to Hastings, Michigan. He told me he had a Sunday car, which he kept in his garage; and every Sunday he would just sit in it and read. He also told me that he and Harold had been brothers all their lives. I always listened and said, "That's good, or nice, Caspert." They were both good and loyal employees, and happy to be working at Bronson.

Good-bye to special friends . . . On January 15, 1965, Mabel Stell Meyle, R.N., retired after 25 years at a time when I was already calling her an old friend. Almost all those who worked as student nurses on Hall 5 (later renamed Hall 6) say that they learned much from and appreciated Mrs. Meyle. It was years later that Betty and I drove to South Haven to say good-bye to Mabel, as she was dying of cancer.

We said good-bye to Gus Lecos in February. He was replaced by Mike Lampos. Gus told him in front of the guys in maintenance, "Take care of these guys, Mike, and they will take care of you." Two years later, when Gus called from Chicago one day, I complained, "I think you'd better tell him again Gus, because he didn't take care of us. We haven't seen a watermelon since you left."

Preventive Maintenance

The Maintenance Department implemented a preventive maintenance program on March 1st. I spent several hours each day deciding which equipment would need inspection and how often. The inspection frequency would be entered into the computer. I worked with Data Processing to determine which forms needed to be filled out, concerning equipment numbers and location of the equipment. When the information came back from Data Processing, it was all printed out in card form and ready to give to the mechanics. When they completed the work, the cards were filed for future reference.

Thanks in appreciation . . . In July the Upjohn Company gave a gift of $300,000 to Bronson for the construction of ten apartment units for residents and interns. These units were built on John Street and were ready for use in the summer of 1969. I was often called to these apartments over the years for one problem or another. It's safe to say that many parties took place at these apartments, with several student nurses in attendance. Seems strange that I never read about them in the *White Caps* yearbooks.

Betty and I attended the Republican National Convention in Miami Beach, Florida, that August. We flew out of Detroit with the Michigan delegation. We had a great time with Governor Romney as leader of our group. Betty and I shook hands with Ronald Reagan, Nelson Rockefeller and Gerald Ford. Richard Nixon was nominated to run against Hubert Humphrey. It was a fun week, but we were glad to be back in Detroit, even if we couldn't remember where we parked our car at the Detroit Metro parking lot. Special thanks to Jo Starkweather for making our trip possible.

After being involved in sports and politics all of my life, I was named to the seven-man Parks and Recreation Commission by the Kalamazoo County Board of Supervisors. I also served as manager of the Nixon campaign for the Third Congressional District. It was a busy time.

Wesley Hall Closed Temporarily

In 1968, Wesley Hall was closed for patient use. The lights were turned off and the doors locked, but I still managed to wander through the halls on occasion, remembering those days when the dorm was filled with nurses. Later, in March of 1969, Bronson established a Hemodialysis Unit on the first floor of Wesley, which would open even later in the year. I was glad that it could be put to another good use.

The Maintenance Department payroll had grown to 18 men, and Plant Operations had ten. There I found myself, writing job evaluations. Sometimes it was difficult to "call it as you see it" on a couple of employees. One nice thing that happened was that Peter Froyd presented a plaque to our department for turning in the greatest number of hospital improvement suggestions. I think that Ray Gurd turned in most of them.

Again, my bad back put me in the hospital on the eighth floor. What worried me more was that the annual Employee Service Award banquet was soon to be held. Since I had never missed an award banquet, I got permission from my doctor to attend on November 12,

The Bronson I Knew

in a wheel chair. I'm thankful the banquet was still held at Harding auditorium so I could go.

As 1969 ended, there were 1,200 full and part-time employees who still enjoyed the hot fudge sundaes in the snack bar (just thought you would like to know that).

~

Late Photo History

Crowning the queen at the Christmas formal, 1960. Left to right: Sue Holben, Kathryn McLeod, Dick Vander Molen, Joan Degoffau.

Dale Duflo and his golden plunger.

Mrs. Kirk and her son, Richard, 1978.

Children's Christmas party in Harding Auditorium, 1964. Left to right: Dorothy Meninga, Hilda Pidgley, Mabel Stell.

BMH softball team. Back row, left to right: Harvey Lehman, Clarence Eigsti, Floyd Miller, Nelson Bushouse, Don Schmidt; middle row: Sam Fitzpatrick, Ralph Meyer, Bill Neiley, Bill Sootsman, Dick Vander Molen; front row, Karl Fortune, Roger Gurgenson, Craig Vander Molen, Dean Troyer, Charlie Leflore.

Late Photo History

Jackie Wylie presenting an honorary diploma from the Bronson Methodist Hospital School of Nursing.

Mabel Stell Meyle and Mr. Dan Finch.

The money tree presented at Theo and Stacey's retiree breakfast.

Earnest Best and me, September 2004.

Boop, Dick, Jayne (Craig's wife), Craig, Steve, and Cheri.

Our Rathburn grandchildren from upper left: Andrew, Joshua, Thomas, Sarah, Emma, Julia.

Our Houghland grandchildren and their parents, left to right: Kate, Hannah, Elizabeth, Debbie, David, David, Abraham, Samuel, Elisha.

Late Photo History

Frank Sardone at a Service Award dinner with the Vander Molens.

Our traveling friends, Dick and Lona Wiessner with Boop.

Our 50th Wedding Anniversary, May 2002.

Dick and Herb Beck at a Service Award dinner, late 1990s.

Beginning demolition of the big dorm, Wesley Hall, 2001.

Boop and Dick in retirement service as hospital escorts.

12
SIGNIFICANT EVENTS OF THE 1970s

1970 was an important year in the history of Bronson Methodist Hospital, which then celebrated the 50th anniversary of its hospital affiliation with the Methodist Church. In February, the new Pediatric–Adolescent building opened. Many employees and student nurses served as hosts and welcomed hundreds of visitors who came to view the new addition. Later in the year, the new Radiology Department opened with Bill Sootsman directing the operations. Every month in the 1970s *The Catalyst* was published for employees and retirees; Russell Watson was editor. It was a publication that we all looked forward to and appreciated, mainly because it was for and about employees.

Finally smoke-free . . . On June 7, the vending machines for cigarettes were removed from all areas of the hospital and Truesdale Hall. The sad thing is that smoking was still permitted in the hospital. A few years later, because so many of us complained, the cafeteria was divided into smoking and non-smoking areas. Finally, 25 years after the removal of the cigarette machines, the hospital became totally smoke-free.

My contact with the student nurses was basically around 4:15 P.M. in the cafeteria where Ward and I had coffee before going home. Dale Duflo had been assigned to work at Truesdale Hall, and he got to know most of the girls.

Church involvement . . . In 1970 Betty and I became youth sponsors at our church. We met every Sunday night with the young people, and every other year we attended the Christian Endeavor convention, no matter where it might be held, from Hawaii to Pennsylvania. It was a rewarding experience for the many years that we served as youth sponsors.

Good news . . . Meetings with the intent of forming an employee union occurred over several weeks. The Michigan Department of Labor set a date for a secret ballot election in Harding Auditorium on November 20. Word came from the MDOL that Bronson employees had voted not to have union representation. I had always been happy with the way Bronson treated and respected its employees and with its benefits program, which was continually reviewed so, for me, the outcome was good news.

Remodeling the diet kitchen meant extending the tray line near the dumb waiters, refrigerators and hot carts. Some outlets need to be relocated and additional outlets installed. Installation of the line was to be completed in one night. Maintenance began the installation at 7:00 P.M. The contractors handled the tray line move, while John and I relocated the outlets. We worked all night and finished just in time for breakfast to be delivered to patients. The next day was a long day for John and me, and we drank lots of coffee to get through it. We were glad when 4:30 P.M. rolled around and we could head for home.

Smitty Appointed Director of Nurses

On January 19, 1971, Hazel Latondress, R.N. received a promotion to director of nursing service. I always remember Smitty, as we called her, as the house supervisor, running up and down the stairs—always on the go. We had a good working relationship, as she was always upbeat and willing to help.

Say it isn't so . . . We received some news from Mr. Finch in February that did not make me very happy, and I know this feeling was shared by many Bronson employees and several Upjohn Company employees. First, we learned that our famous snack bar would be closed. It had been used since 1950 for employees, visitors, and yes, Upjohn Company employees. Hot fudge sundaes, sandwiches, coffee and cakes, etc. would come to an end. For employees, a new lounge on the second floor of Harding building would be serving coffee and rolls only. For doctors, a dining room would be located near the Wesley Hall basement. Visitors would be allowed to use the cafeteria. The other sad news was the closing of Harding gym, so it could become a locker room for male employees. Harding gym, before it was used for Bronson sports teams, was my gym, or so I would like to think. I would take my kids there and we would play basketball almost every Saturday.

Best news . . . Some very good news came in May when Bristol (Brit) Messer was appointed administrative assistant, reporting to W.E. Johnson. Brit had been working in the Personnel Department. Before Mr. Finch's announcement came out, Brit and I were in Lansing, Michigan, at a safety seminar. During lunch break we walked over to the Capitol building where he told me of his promotion and that maintenance would be one of the areas of his responsibility. I replied that was the best news I could wish for. Brit and I had a great working relationship. He was by far the most reasonable, understanding, and fair administrator that I ever reported to. It was a sad day later when he left for Missouri and was replaced by James K. Stroebel.

In June, Paul Lechner decided to take early retirement and was replaced as assistant supervisor by my long-time friend Ralph Stewart. On his last day, Paul took off his watch, put in on the anvil, hit it with a hammer and said, "That's the last time that I will keep track of time."

Long-time employee and director of the pharmacy, Kenneth Huckendubler, was appointed administrative assistant, also reporting to W.E. Johnson. From August 1983–1986, I would report to Ken.

Significant Events of the 1970s

More Construction

More parking space and more doctor offices were needed, so in September construction began for the parking ramp on the corner of Lovell and Jasper streets and the West Medical Center office building on Lovell Street. Of course, this meant more work for the maintenance crew and hiring of more men. Also, more interviews, more evaluations and a few more anticipated headaches.

By July 1972, the new intern's residence on Dutton Street was ready for the arrival of the new interns, in addition to the homes built a few years earlier. I told Ray Gurd, when he left the shop for the intern quarters in September, to catch a bus because of the distance from our shop to Dutton Street, "Only kidding."

Work started in the summer, on the destruction of the old loading dock, where a new surgery unit and cafeteria would be located. No one could enter through the back door, where at one time the one-room, emergency room was located. I watched the work proceed from the sun porch on 2 East when I had the chance, and I remembered the scene when the student nurses sat on the dock while taking a break from class.

Although I haven't mentioned it for awhile, I haven't forgotten the many classes that had graduated during the past five years. The 70 girls in the class of '72 held their graduation exercises on April 26. They seemed to be graduating earlier and earlier every year.

201

The Bronson I Knew

Keep your feet off my desk! John Filler joined the Bronson family as the assistant food manager. I always enjoyed John, even when he came to my office with a maintenance request and sat in a chair putting his feet on my desk—just to see my reaction. I didn't say anything—until now.

One of the many non-maintenance jobs I was asked to do, and enjoyed, was to play Santa Claus at the Christmas parties. Often I went to the children's rooms after the employee party was over, still dressed all in fur from my head to my foot, to see how excited the kids were to see Santa and, if the nurse said it was OK, receive a candy cane.

Of the Four Horsemen, I'm the only one left . . . In 1973, Ralph Stewart, whom I had the privilege of working with for 26 years, retired. It seemed strange to no longer have Ralph, Roy and Floyd around for their friendship and advice. We were the four who, during the 1940s and most of the 1950s, ran the Maintenance Department.

The Maintenance Department had held their annual Fish Fry in March, for the past five years. We had three or four ice fishermen in the department. We invited many of our special friends throughout the hospital to join us for lunch. Dr. Ajemian was one of the first one of those special friends. This particular year, the menu included fish, lemon salad, French bread, dill pickles, homemade cake and coffee or milk.

Significant Events of the 1970s

The only thing better than the annual Fish Fry, was our yearly Christmas party, which was held in our shop for all of the hospital employees. It was the only time we cleaned our shop, and it took us a whole day to set up for the fun. Christmas was a party that employees looked forward to each year, as over 200 were served a fabulous lunch.

Peds Expands

In late fall of 1974, two more floors were added to the Peds building, as we called it. The fourth floor was for OB, and the Upjohn Company used the fifth floor. At the open house, I was one of four department heads to serve as a host, along with the student nurses.

At the Service Awards banquet held in November, a man showed up whom I didn't know. Most of those in attendance didn't realize who he was either. Finally someone yelled, "It's Dale Duflo with a wig on." We all had a good laugh as Dale took off his wig and looked bald once again. He was the highlight of the evening. I received my 30-year award from Daniel Finch—only ten more to go.

Ward stepped down as Plant Superintendent in December of 1974, replaced by James Hoffman the next year. Ward remained as supervisor in charge of the preventive maintenance program. My title was changed to Plant Maintenance manager, and I had 35 maintenance employees reporting to me as department head.

On March 25, I met with my crew and informed them that the new Surgery Department was about to open on April 7. We needed to do several things to help. Starting on Friday, April 4, from 4:00–9:00 P.M. and on Saturday and Sunday from 7:00 A.M. until the move was complete, many things were to be done, for example, the Skytron light and the XO mat, as well as all of the other equipment, needed checks before being used. I put Jim Stevens in charge of this project. The job was done well, and surgery opened as planned on schedule.

Nice to be of help . . . One of the more gratifying aspects of my job as the manager of the Maintenance Department was to be able to help employees from other departments in the hospital join the maintenance crew. Many came from dietary, laundry and housekeeping. Most turned out to be good employees, grateful for the opportunity to advance. Many are still working in the Maintenance Department in 2004. One such employee is Chuck Barnett, who worked in the dietary department and is now the hospital locksmith. Many others hold important positions with the Maintenance Department. Dan Kettenbiel, who started his employment at the hospital as a painter's helper, is now the director of physical facilities. Ken Powell, Project Manager, is the one person that contractors and architects have always sought for advice. His love for Bronson is almost as great as mine. Jim Stevens, now retired, was my right hand man for many years as the maintenance manager. Henry Sopjes, Hugh Graham and Ted Musselman, all now retired, were supervisors whose advice and expertise I relied on. To all of these employees and many more, I'll always be grateful.

Bronson's 75th Birthday

Bronson celebrated its 75th anniversary in 1975. The guys in the shop celebrated with cake from the bakery and our own brewed coffee. It seemed like we were willing to celebrate almost anything as long as food was involved.

One of the organizations I belonged to was the Southwestern Michigan Hospital Association of Engineers. Omer, Ward and I were charter members way back in 1966. Omer served as president in 1967. Ward was president in 1972, and in 1975 it was my turn. Once a month we met at various hospitals, had speakers and discussed our mutual problems. Over the years I have kept in touch with the organization and especially the men I associated with.

In 1976 our department worked on a lot of remodeling projects throughout the hospital and medical centers. For me, this required more paper work. One department job I always seemed to end up getting was to be a captain for the United Way. I have never liked to ask people for money, but I told myself it was for a good cause.

Nurses from the Philippines . . . November 1976 brought word that 30 Filipino nurses were coming to Bronson. I met with Ken Huckendubler on 2 West to learn that we would house these nurses in patient rooms. Ray Gurd then put locks on all of the patient rooms, and we awaited the nurses' arrival—probably in December. A call went out to anyone who would like to donate boots or winter coats (small size only), it would be appreciated. Several employees answered the call, and many coats and boots are brought into the hospital. Hazel Latondress and her staff worked with the Philippine nurses who were assigned to different areas of the hospital. Then, with less than three months on the job, 2 West was completely empty of nurses. They left during the early morning hours without telling anyone. We never found out why they left or where they went.

In 1977 Bronson had 2,246 employees. During this year, the ninth and tenth floors were converted into patient use, eliminating our being able to store so many items on these floors. Where to put all the things that found a home on Halls 9 and 10, was a puzzle for years, but I believe most of it was junked.

I found myself as a member of the Energy Committee chaired by Jim Hoffman in 1977. This committee required many meetings and a lot of my time. Also, I served for four years, on the hospital Purchasing Service that met once a month in Middleville, Michigan. In the warm months it was a nice ride, but it gets a little slippery in the winter on the back roads.

Significant Events of the 1970s

Blizzard Once More

We all thought that the blizzard of 1967 was bad, but then came the blizzard of '78, and most of us said, "Here we go again." Our thanks heartily went to the student nurses who worked those four days, helping at the nursing stations, laundry, dietary or wherever else they were needed. The rest of us, who were stranded once again, also did whatever other tasks remained to be done. I'm thankful that this year had the last blizzard of my working days at Bronson.

The Maintenance Department—I had used that name for years when answering the telephone. It meant Floyd, Roy, Ralph, Dick, Clark, Jack, Dale, Ray, John and so many others. With the changing times, we became known instead as the Physical Facilities Department. Other departments throughout the hospital also experienced new names in what was called progress. A secretary now answered the phone, but it was still and always will be—our maintenance department to me—even if not by that name.

Former logo . . . The Bronson English-style "B," which we associated with Bronson for so many years, was replaced by a new logo in September. Although the official hospital stationery would no longer display the familiar "B," the nursing school alumni voted to continue using it. Thank you, alums, I have always loved that Bronson "B."

The Bronson I Knew

In November, after 28 years of being director of Bronson Methodist Hospital School of Nursing, Helen Weber, retired. Many students made it through training because of Mrs. Weber's encouragement. When I saw her a year after she retired and asked what she was doing with her time, she replied, "Going back to school."

Jackie, Russ and Dale . . . I remember Jackie Wylie as a student nurse, coming into training in 1959 as a freshman, when I was the manager of the Bronson White Caps sports teams. Jackie always promised me she would come out to watch us play, but she never did. But I forgave her years ago, "Right Jackie?" On December 1, 1978, upon Mrs. Weber's retirement, this Bronson graduate received a promotion as her replacement.

One day, Russ Watson asked if I would give him a hand on Wednesday nights, operating the Civil Defense emergency radio from a small kitchen on the seventh floor. This I did for several years, until I asked Jim Kostakis to take over for me—another instance of finding my own replacement before being able to quit. Nevertheless, it was good spending Wednesday nights at home once again.

Dale Duflo, who worked for me for nearly 20 years, retired May 1, 1979. Dale was the man who repaired the pneumatic tube system. Sometimes I had to call him in at night to repair the system, and he always came. He was well liked by the student nurses; Dale always carried a plunger around to unplug the girls' tubs. He faithfully did this, year after year. At his retirement party, we presented Dale with a golden plunger.

Andy Vander Molen, my big brother, who had worked at Bronson since 1957, retired from the Maintenance Department the first of August 1979. He worked as a mechanic on the 11:00 P.M. to 7:00 A.M. shift. Andy told more Dutch jokes than I did, and my dog Jiggs, was his gift to me. In 1938, he took me to Detroit to watch a Tigers ballgame. As the church team's batboy, I always rode to the church baseball games with him. Andy was away in the service for nearly five years during World War II. I wrote to him often and was thankful when he returned home safely after the war. I really missed him.

Golden Anniversary

Bronson Methodist Hospital School of Nursing celebrated its 75th anniversary at Truesdale Hall on Saturday, May 19, 1979. Commemorations took place at Truesdale Hall in the morning and at Western Michigan University Student Center that evening. Mary B. Anderson, Helen Weber and Lyle Nottingham were special guests. When Mary B. was introduced, she received a standing ovation. She sat next to Mr. Finch, the person who was responsible for the loss of her job at Bronson. I think that I applauded the loudest—I was so pleased for Miss Anderson. Several in attendance yelled, "Have Dick stand," and when I did, they all stood up again and applauded some more. I noticed Miss Anderson standing and clapping with the rest of the people. I was really overwhelmed by their response. It was a great night, with several hundred in attendance.

Energy Committee chair retires . . . Jim Hoffman and I spent a good deal of time together at the architect's office of T.P.T. (Tower, Pinkster and Titus), as well as in meetings and early mornings in the chapel for prayer—we felt we needed it. We traveled to many engineering seminars around the country. As chairman of the Energy Committee, he had saved the hospital a great deal of money. He left Bronson in early 1985, and retired to his summer home at Gun Lake.

One day, the cafeteria cashier said, "Dick, you don't smile any more, and you always used to." Boy, did that ever jar me. It must have been the pressure of the job. Smiling was one of my trademarks. Whenever I would meet an employee I would always say, "Hey, hi, hello there," always smiling.

During my lunch hours, I would walk downtown, just to get a break from the pressures at work. Many times I would wander through the F.W. Woolworth Co. on Burdick Street. I remember as a kid, my sister Elsie and I caught a bus to go shopping downtown, and Woolworth's was always one of our stops. At the end of 1979 Woolworth would close its store, the beginning of the end to downtown, as we knew it.

~

13
EARLY 1980s — RETIREMENT AHEAD

Leaving the hospital at 3:30 P.M., and walking to the parking lot with my son, Steve, who was working at Bronson's Central Distribution, it started raining before we got to the car. Then we noticed how dark the sky looked. We drove home in a downpour with the wind blowing wildly. It was May 13, 1980, the day that a tornado went through downtown Kalamazoo. Betty was working in the medical center for OB-Gyn. She, along with everyone in the doctor's office, headed for the basement. That day none of us will ever forget, especially the crew in ER. They treated over 66 people.

At the Service Awards annual banquet held on Armistice Day at the Kalamazoo Center, I received my 35-year award from Daniel Finch. I shared the spotlight with Hazel Latondress, Maxine Clark and Karyle Ketchum, who received their 30-year awards.

Hospital Growth

During 1981 Bronson Methodist Hospital continued to grow. While extensive remodeling of Halls 4 and 6 occurred, I spent many hours going over a checklist to make sure everything was completed. In May, Ken Huckendubler named Herb Beck as director of Environmental Services. Herb and I made hospital rounds together and he became my lunch partner and friend. Over the years we had lunch many times at Gilmore's department store. Herb would often stop and play the grand piano on Gilmore's first floor by the escalator before we left, as customers looked and wondered who we were.

In 1983, I was promoted to director of Plant Operations. Bronson's new, Genevieve U. and Donald S. Gilmore Center for Health Education was dedicated that June. Located on Pine Street (now Healthcare Plaza) on the site of the former Zion Lutheran Church, this building was the site of many, many meetings I would attend.

A new landing pad was completed in August, ready for its first use the following month. A crowd gathered to watch the Care Flight helicopter land.

Crosstown Center, the old Sears Building a few blocks south, became Bronson's new Outpatient Surgery facility. It opened in December 1983, yet another area of responsibility for the maintenance crew. In the summer, I enjoyed the walk to Crosstown Center, but I drove my car in the winter. Bronson Healthcare Group had purchased The Crosstown Inn, formerly a Holiday Inn, as additional parking was needed for Outpatient Surgery.

Contracts were then let out to tear down Crosstown Inn for 400 parking spaces instead of this motel.

1984 was a year to remember for various reasons. Many changes, especially in administration, were about to take place. Bronson Healthcare Group continued to expand with Mr. Finch as chairman; Russell P. Kneen, president; and William A. Johnson, vice-president. Peter Froyd was then president of Bronson Methodist Hospital. This was the last year of the dual administration of Daniel Finch and Peter Froyd. Those of us who were there appreciated their leadership over all the many years.

Old entrance . . . The hospital entrance on Lovell Street, which had been built in 1950 and was known as the "1950 entrance," closed on April 5, 1985. A new lobby and courtyard were opened. This beautiful new lobby will only have a lifespan of some 18 years, whereupon a *New* Bronson at 601 John Street will open for business. I can still remember running up the seven steps of the old entrance and going out through the swinging doors for lunch at Holly's, on the corner of Burdick and Lovell streets.

After 24 years as Bronson's president and later chairman of the board of BHG, Mr. Finch retired in July 1985. I felt honored that at his retirement dinner, I was asked to give a speech on behalf of the employees. During the course of my talk I reminded him of that day, long ago, when in the hospital lobby as I was looking over at him, he asked, "Do I know you?"

I had replied, "No, but it probably would be a good idea if you did." The hundreds of people in attendance had a good laugh.

Early Retirement Plan Offered

Big news in 1985, happened in late November for some 86 Bronson employees. We learned that the hospital would be offering early retirement as an early Christmas present and, probably, our best one. For those of us who were eligible for early retirement the Personnel Department called us in for an explanation of our options. When it was my turn, Rick Geer said, "Dick, you have two weeks to think about whether you would like to retire and, if you decide to retire, you will need to sign these papers."

"Rick," I said, "give me your pen and show me where to sign. I don't need two weeks to think about it. I'm ready to take early retirement." I was 56 years old and had been employed at Bronson for nearly 41 years. At the Service Awards banquet in November 1985, I received my 40-year award, the last one I was to receive.

In January 1986 many of us who took early retirement, had only one more month to work. There seemed to be so many things I wanted to do and people to see before retiring. In the middle of the month, Ken Huckendubler hired my replacement, then—at the last minute—he changed his mind. Administration asked me if I would stay on for one more year. My answer was no.

I felt ready to leave. I told them that Jim Stevens and Ken Powell could handle the job.

My Last Week at Bronson

The last week of January 1986, was my last week to work. On Monday morning, I said to my secretary, Jean, "I'm afraid this week is going to go by too fast." As usual I had several meetings on Monday. At night, a dinner reception was held for eight of my fellow workers in the Maintenance Department, who also took advantage of early retirement.

Tuesday I spent the day packing all my belongings of nearly 41 years (I never threw anything away). Wednesday, I was still packing and started saying a few good-byes. That night, the guys in the shop gave me a retirement party—a farewell dinner at the Birches. One hundred and sixty people, including the Maintenance Department employees and my family attended it. Needless to say, I was too excited to eat.

Many readers will remember that at our big table in the cafeteria, I would rather talk to them than eat, and so it was that night. I was presented with many gifts: a VCR with 10 free movies, a beautiful plaque engraved with a picture of Bronson as it looked when I started to work there in 1945 and a picture as it looked on my retirement date; two beautiful jackets, one from the Bronson softball team (I was still playing ball at age 56) and one from Western Michigan University; two beautiful, leather-bound photo albums with so many pictures, from early days to present. I wish you could all see them. Also presented to me were candy, plants, checks, etc. Several employees spoke during the evening and my daughter, Cheryl, sang two songs. Needless to say, when it came my turn to speak, I had a tear or two in my eyes and a lump in my throat. During that week I didn't sleep very much and this night was no exception. It was a great night, and I am thankful for all the fine gifts I received.

Thursday found me still packing up my things. It was taking me longer than I thought because if I came across a picture I would sit and daydream about days long since passed and wonder where all those years had gone. I realized that I was no longer Dick the buffer or Dick the electrician. Bill Sootsman, who was director of Radiology, had also taken early retirement and that night I spoke at his retirement dinner.

Friday, January 31 was a sad day in a way. I made a final tour of the hospital on that day. I saved the old dorm where many special memories I hold dear abound until last. Along with the old dorm, I also had many special memories of North Home, South Home, East Home, Pine Home and Truesdale Hall, most having fallen victim to the wrecking ball.

On my last day of work, a 2:00 P.M. reception was held for me in the Gilmore Center, just south of Truesdale Hall, that included a large cake, which said, "Mr. Bronson". It really touched me. After speeches from Peter Froyd and Russ Kneen, who said, "I knew the day Dick retired would be a dramatic occasion, but I

Early 1980s — Retirement Ahead

didn't know we would have an earthquake at noontime," which, of course we did. The big surprise of the day came when Jackie Wylie presented me with an honorary diploma from the Bronson School of Nursing. That was really exciting and how proud I was. That really meant a lot to me, and still to this day, I show it off to my friends.

My wife Betty, sons, Steve and Craig, and daughter, Cheryl and Craig's wife, Jayne, stood in a reception line with me. I was overwhelmed by the hundreds of people who turned out to say good-bye. At 3:30 P.M. several people spoke and were very kind in their remarks. When the time came to leave, with my family to help with the gifts, we drove off toward home, leaving so many memories of the past 41 years behind.

At the Bronson alumni dinner in February 1986, I was a guest of honor. It was great to see and reminisce with friends about the special days we shared. The alums presented me with a beautiful plaque, which reads:

MAN ON THE FLOOR AWARD
TO
DICK VANDER MOLEN

Our MAN ON THE FLOOR, in gratitude for
Unfailing smiles, support and service to approximately
2,000 BMH School of Nursing students during nearly 41 years
of listening, understanding, helping, encouraging,
and remembering us as individuals.
We return in full measure, our loving wishes for a long and
Rewarding retirement.
Presented February 12, 1986

This plaque hangs proudly in our home. Thank you too, alumni, for the many other gifts, especially the season tickets for Western's football and basketball games that fall. The box of cards and the notes and letters from *my* nurses all over the United States brought tears to my eyes as I spent several hours reading every word and remembering all the events they wrote about. It will come as no surprise that my happiest days at Bronson were spent talking with them either in the cafeteria, dorm or on the floors. Even now I find myself looking over the many yearbooks, recalling the fun and good times.

~

14
RETIREMENT BEGINS

Betty and I took a three-week vacation to Florida toward the end of February. I kept thinking about what my desk would look like when I got back. Then reality set in, and I realized that I was retired. In April, I had shoulder surgery, making me a patient on the west end of Hall 6 for five days. I had lots of company, and it seemed like old times.

I have been a member of the American Society for Hospital Engineering for many years. For its annual convention to be held in Grand Rapids in the summer of 1987, the convention committee asked me if I would be responsible for free-time activities for the wives and others attending the convention. Being retired, I checked this out with Bronson's administration, which consented to send me to San Diego for a week in September 1986, to meet with the convention committee. The hospital also paid my expenses for the convention in Grand Rapids that lasted for five days. I was very appreciative to administration for allowing me to attend.

The Bronson I Knew

Betty, who worked in the OB-Gyn office for 24 years, retired in the summer of 1987. We then traveled with our church friends, Dick and Lona Wiessner, over the next 15 years. We went south and east, but never west.

Retiree Activities

After meeting with Rick Geer in the Personnel Department, I asked his advice on starting a retiree's newsletter. He gave me the use of some space in his department, and the *Bronson Retirees' Newsletter* was born. Our first publication was dated November 1986 and it is still published every other month for Bronson retirees and retired doctors.

Next, I started a monthly breakfast, which meets the first Monday of every month for retirees and doctors. Since we were a close group of employees during our workdays at Bronson, I thought, why not continue meeting over breakfast? We have had great turnouts each month.

John Baas, the personnel manager, and I were talking in his office one day, and we both agreed that the hospital needed to start an escort service to help visitors find their way around the hospital. Bill Sootsman, Hazel Latondress, and I volunteered to do this once a week. All three of us are still at it, but now in the *New* Bronson.

I can usually be found on the second floor of the Medical Office Pavilion every Wednesday morning, while

Boop is on the first floor with her friendly smile, greeting and helping visitors. On Thursday's she cuddles babies in the Neo-Natal Intensive Care Unit. For those of us who volunteer, we appreciate Julie and Sue for their helpful ways and encouragement over these many years, especially at the annual volunteer appreciation banquet, and to Bronson Methodist Hospital for its recognition of the many volunteers who give of their time in numerous areas of the hospital.

First Reformed Church

I have attended and been a member of the First Reformed Church for 75 years. It was located on the corner of Church and Academy streets, across from beautiful Bronson Park. My family attended church service twice every Sunday; in the morning for church service and Sunday school, and then the evening service from 7:00–8:00 P.M. Family night was on Thursday, and catechism on Saturday morning. This was my regular routine as I was growing up. We rode to church in two cars, except during the war years, when we mostly walked, as did so many others.

I remember the programs at Christmas time when we, as children, would put on a play or speak some part, and sing as a group. It was something I really wasn't crazy about doing, but I didn't have a choice. The Sunday school picnics at Long Lake were something we all looked forward to. In later years they were held at Milham Park. When I was in my twenties, I served as assistant Sunday school superintendent.

In later years, Betty and I served as youth leaders in Christian Endeavor. We met every Sunday night, after church, each time in different homes. Every other year, starting in 1979, we traveled to many places to the International Christian Endeavor conventions. These included trips to Canada and Holland, Michigan, by car; to Maine, Hawaii, and Oregon by plane, to Indiana and New York by bus, and to Pennsylvania by train. There were always fund-raising projects going on. These included car washes, serving breakfasts and dinners, and raking leaves. Our congregation always supported us and we were always able to take 30 or more kids on these trips, along with several sponsors.

After Craig and his wife, Jayne, took over the Christian Endeavor program, Betty and I served on the consistory for many years. I first served as a deacon and later as an elder. Betty served as elder and chaired several committees. Most of these later years I was the church property chairman, along with all the headaches that a 150-year-old building can produce. Betty and I also volunteered in the Vine neighborhood, working with the children on Tuesday afternoons.

For years, I drove my car and made two trips, to bring unchurched kids to Sunday school and church. Later, after someone donated a van, I could usually make only one trip. I learned it was important to be involved with kids, not just on Sundays, so Betty and I would sometimes take them to breakfast or lunch during the week, go to things at their school, take them out for their birthdays, and let them know we cared about them. It was truly a rewarding experience.

Over the years, the attendance in our church began to decline. A tough decision was made. On the last Sunday in December of 2003, we closed our downtown doors. During our final service, many former members returned to help us say good-bye. Many tears were shed, as we reminisced about the former days and the ministers and friends we all knew. Almost all of the remaining members joined the Second Reformed Church on Stadium Drive, which Betty and I now call our church home.

Chase Golf Balls?

I always told people that I would never waste my time chasing a little white golf ball. After we retired, Gordon Roberts and Dick Wiessner asked me to join them for breakfast. I said, "Great, where are we going?"

"To the Colonial Kitchen on Drake Road," they said. That was my first mistake, because after breakfast, I found myself in Gordon's car headed for the golf course. They had an extra set of clubs for me to use and the rest is history. I've been golfing ever since.

During the past 18 years, we have met every Tuesday for breakfast and nine holes of golf. Howard Boshoven, Roger Schultz, Dick Nap, Paul Kleis, Bob Thompson, and Bob Mickey, who because of death or health reasons are no longer able to play, joined us over the years. Our group now includes Tom Veld, Louie Hecker, Mark Walvoord, Roland Springgate, Dean Richardson, Bob Bellis and Bob Bouserman. We play many different courses within 50 miles of Kalamazoo. The only one of us to ever sink a hole-in-one was Bob Thompson, and that was several years ago. He celebrated by buying breakfast for everyone. The rest of us keep trying and because I don't think we will ever match Bob's hole-in-one, I supply the guys with a candy nip if they par a hole. I sure have a lot of candy nips left.

After Betty retired, she also took up the game of golf. We usually play together once or twice a week. For many years we played with Dick and Lona Wiessner and took golf vacations with them. Recently Betty joined a women's golf league and plays every Friday morning.

Helping Alumni

Conducting tours for BMH nursing classes celebrating 25-, 35- and 50-year class reunions is something we both enjoy. Betty and I attend many class reunions. Often the question, "Dick, what was your favorite class?" is asked. My answer always is that it is the class whose reunion we are attending. This makes everyone happy. I guess I should have been a politician. Now, if you really want to know. . . . Although it was always fun giving tours of the big dorm and the 10-story hospital, we are just as eager to show off the *New* Bronson.

Over the years while working, and later in retirement, I always found myself helping with the annual alumni bazaar. First it was held off from the Lovell Street lobby. Marie McLeieer would call me a month ahead of time and ask for my help. She would call again during the week before the sale and also on the night before. "I'll be there," I always assured her.

The front lobby of the hospital was a great place for the sale, as we had many visitors. We probably made more money in this location than in any of the locations in future years. I always made rounds around the hospital to remind everyone to come to the bazaar. Even now, some 25 years later, Marie calls and says, "Dick, see you at 7:00 A.M. to unload for the bazaar—OK?"

"Marie, I'll be there." It's a fun time and I really do enjoy doing it.

Being an honorary member of the Bronson alumni, I always attend the semi-annual alumni meetings with Betty. For me, it's another fun time to visit with the girls. I remember them so many years ago, coming into training with frightened looks on their faces. We always have a nice brunch, a program and great fellowship. I can't help but wonder why more graduates don't support their association and join us at these meetings.

I've also enjoyed writing in the alumni *Bulletin* for many years. More important to me is reading the letters from the alumni and to hear about them and their families.

Job Losses

Three years after I retired, Bronson eliminated 50 jobs. Many of my friends and many faithful employees lost their jobs, through no fault of their own. The following week, on April 18, Peter Froyd, the hospital president and Ed Spartz, corporate vice president, were let go. In June, 206 more positions were eliminated. It reminded me of a few years earlier when I had to tell eight other employees that their jobs had been eliminated. They were to turn in their keys and leave immediately. It was very difficult for me. They were all good workers. How sorry I was to have to tell them this news. Several took it very hard. I had tears in my own eyes.

In August 1988 we invited more than 50 Amish residents from northern Indiana to attend our retirees' picnic behind Truesdale Hall. It was good to see so many and meet their families. These people had been classified I-W by the draft board, and had worked their two-year commitment at Bronson. We ate some great Amish food and reminisced all afternoon. Years later, Betty and I attended one of their own reunions in South Bend.

From word received from Ormond, Florida in February 1992, we learned that Mary H. Perdew had died at age 94. Her husband was Dr. William Perdew, who died in 1960. Most of the nurses working on 2 East remembered Mrs. Perdew for the care she gave her mother while in room 230 for a period of several years. I knew Mrs. Perdew too. We often talked about the hospital and the changes that were taking place, until she moved from Kalamazoo in 1985.

When Russell Kneen stepped down as CEO and chairman of Bronson Healthcare Group, Patric Ludwig assumed the position. He later asked me to serve on some special committees. It was sort of nice to be involved once again and to be able to contribute.

Frank Sardone Promoted

On September 1, 1994, Pat Ludwig announced that Frank Sardone would assume the new role of executive vice president and chief operating officer. Frank is a "people person" and was well received by the employees.

Finding Earnest Best... Herb Beck called me at home one day and told me about a man he had met who worked in the Bronson laundry during the early 1940s. He said his name was Earnest Best, and he wondered if I knew him. I said, "No, but I would like to meet him."

"Too late," Herb said, "he left for his home in Des Plains, Arkansas." I was eager to talk to Mr. Best, so in a few days I called him and we talked for nearly an hour. We planned to meet the next time he came to Kalamazoo. When he arrived in Herb's office, he called me and I met them for lunch. Afterwards, I took Earnest for a tour of what would have been the laundry and located his office, now used as a storeroom. We talked about the employees that we both knew who worked in the laundry, as well as about his boss, Karl Gibson, whom we both appreciated.

Earnest told me that when he left Bronson, he had recommended Harvey Meyers to replace him in the laundry. Over the years, Earnest and I have met for lunch on many occasions. He has written several books and in one of his books, he included a chapter about his days at Bronson Methodist Hospital. He has given me all of his books, and I consider Earnest a friend and faithful retired department head of the Laundry Department.

Losing dear friends . . . Ralph Stewart was a patient at Bronson for a week in August 1995. I visited Ralph each day and knew that he was very sick. I did most of the talking as I reminisced about our days in the maintenance shop. He smiled and I knew he enjoyed hearing about those days once again. On Wednesday morning, August 9, Ralph passed away. He was not only proud to have been a part of the Bronson team, he was proud of his family and his Lord, whom he loved so very much. He was proud to share that love with all of us. We can all be thankful to Ralph for the many photos he snapped over the years, which he gave me to share with readers of the retirees' newsletter. All of us are blessed for having known Ralph.

On May 30, 1996, Pat Ludwig passed away unexpectedly. He had planned to retire later in the year. Frank Sardone replaced him as president and CEO of

Bronson Healthcare Group. Under Frank's leadership, Bronson would receive many national awards. Frank reminds me a lot of Dr. Perdew, who was also a "people person." Their only difference is that Dr. Perdew was an ordained minister and Frank is not, but I think he would make a good one.

The New Bronson reconfigures whole blocks downtown . . . At the corner of Burdick and Dutton streets, I gathered along with employees, retirees, volunteers and maybe a few doctors to celebrate the ground breaking for the *New* Bronson Methodist Hospital on October 4, 1996. A 750-space parking structure would be the first phase of the campus project. As I looked around, I remembered all the houses, including the resident and interns building, that once lined the streets. Two or three houses were saved and moved to Westnedge Avenue.

In the spring of 1997, we say good-bye to an old friend, Truesdale Hall. The dream of so many and show place for student nurses would soon give way to the wrecking ball. Truesdale Hall, in 1957, opened its doors for the first time to student nurses. Many of us remember its spacious rooms for students to study, and sleep, etc., its beautiful lounge and recreation room. Students had enjoyed a safe and comfortable life at Truesdale for over 40 too-short years. A few days before the doors were locked for good, several former students and I walked its halls for the last time. Demolition of this building will not dim memories, the laughter and the tears of those who lived there.

The Bronson I Knew

The last class of Bronson Methodist Hospital School of Nursing had been meeting on the fifth floor of the Peds building for classes their final year. Sadly, more than 60 people who wanted to attend BMH School of Nursing in 1999 would have to look elsewhere.

Special events . . . On May 1, 1998, the 95th graduating class held its commencement exercises at the First United Methodist Church where every seat was filled. On Saturday, May 2, at the Radisson Hotel, alumni gathered in the morning for a program, reminiscing and class reunions. At one point in the program, Betty and I were called to the stage area and presented with gifts from the alumni who wanted to recall those days when I was the "man on the floor." It was great to see so many girls from the different classes and to once again, from the stage, yell "Man on the floor."

In the afternoon I arranged for ten tour guides to escort groups through the hospital and the dorm (Wesley Hall). That night the program was called "Legacy of Caring: Past, Present and Future." What a night to remember! Frank Sardone opened the cornerstone capsule from Truesdale Hall. I remembered the day that those items were placed there. None of us wanted the night to end, but end it must, as the nurses sang their Alma Mater.

The good news for all Bronson alumni was that in May 1999, Western Michigan University's School of Nursing was named the Bronson School of Nursing at

Western Michigan University. Over the previous five years, Bronson had given $5.25 million to WMU's School of Nursing.

After the BMH School of Nursing closed, we noticed a big change at the hospital. No longer were the halls filled with student nurses. It seemed so strange, after all the years with student nurses everywhere. They were the core of nursing care and given great responsibilities. They were proud of the excellent training they received, and almost with the blink of an eye, both they and the old hospital they served so well are gone. A *New* Bronson has taken the place of the old Bronson, as it is now referred to. Other people have taken the place of Bronson's students, but it can never be the same again.

On November 22, 1998, Betty and I had volunteered to be tour guides in the *New* Bronson. We attended a tour guide orientation session on December 6 a year later. We were told to wear flat, hard-soled shoes and a hard hat supplied by the Maintenance Department. The tours were still five or six months away. We received a book of instructions to read in the meantime. What better way to spend cold winter nights?

The *New* Bronson

In April 2000, the doctor's office building opened as part of Phase 2 in construction of the new hospital. The building also included outpatient services and the Sky Court Café. We eagerly await the completion of Phase 3,

The Bronson I Knew

the opening of the *New* Bronson, scheduled to open December 4, 2000.

Right on schedule, the *New* Bronson opened, and patients were moved to the new hospital via the tunnel. All went well. I did not help with the move, but was on standby if needed. I found myself wandering through the empty old hospital's lonely halls at least once a week, until the building was torn down. I remembered the people and events that took place during its 50-year existence.

My main concern during this time was trying to save Wesley Hall. I thought it could be turned into a historical museum where all of Bronson's archives could be put on display. I went to Frank Sardone and asked if we could save it. He listened compassionately, but said it would cost too much to remove the asbestos and bring Wesley up to code. I thanked him for his time. This beautiful building with all the history of nearly 100 years would soon be history itself.

When the day of demotion arrived, I sat in a chair across the street from the hospital every day for an entire week, and watched as the building was leveled to the ground. The *Kalamazoo Gazette* interviewed me about my memories when I worked in the dorm at Wesley Hall. The story made the front page of the *Gazette*. Everyone would know how much this building and the many past events have meant to me. With the demolition of the Medical West building on Lovell Street, only Harding Building remains, along with the Medical Center East building and Peds building on the north campus. Plans for this area are a green space with some additional parking. Those "good old days" at Bronson are ones we all hold dear and can never be taken away.

January 21, 2001, marked Bronson's 100-year of service to Kalamazoo. At the retirees' breakfast we joined in the celebration with a large happy birthday cake and song. Bronson Methodist Hospital then entered its second Century of Caring. At the age of 75, I looked back at my 60 years at Bronson, remembering how fortunate I've been to be a part of the Bronson family for so long. I also looked forward to being of service until my retirement anniversary in 2014 at the age of 85.

Our Wedding Anniversary

Betty and I celebrated our 50th wedding anniversary on May 10, 2002. Our three children and daughter-in-law made arrangements in the Bronson Gilmore Center, and guests came from near and far. As we had met at Bronson and spent a great deal of our lives there, what better place to celebrate? We were overwhelmed with the turnout and to see so many of our relatives and friends. It was another day to remember.

Boop and I don't have any grandchildren of our own, but feel very blessed to have 13 adopted grandchildren. Our former pastor, Van Rathburn and his wife, Terry, have three boys and three girls who call us grandma and grandpa. Although they now live in Sioux Center, Iowa, we manage to get together once a year.

233

Letters and phone calls help bring us closer, especially on birthdays. Our other seven adopted grandchildren belong to David and Debbie Houghland. They have three girls and four boys, and live in Kalamazoo. It's always a joy when we get together, but especially for birthday parties, and we hear them say, "Hi, grandma and grandpa." Thank you Lord, for bringing these two families into our lives.

Portrait painter . . . Dr. Donald May, a good friend for many years, took up painting as a hobby. He shares his paintings with the retirees at our breakfast get-togethers. One such painting is that of Dr. Sid Heersma, long time pediatrician. At one of our breakfasts, he told me, "Dick, you are next on my list to have your picture painted." Naturally, I'm honored. We met at my home on several occasions and then he surprised all of us, including me, when he brought his painting of me to the retiree breakfast. He showed the painting which he had named, "Caring Hands," to all of us, and that large portrait now hangs proudly in our living room. Thank you, Dr. May.

Looking Back at the Harding Building

When Harding School first opened in 1927, my brother Andy was one of the first students to attend. Later my sister, Gert, also attended. Later when Bronson rented two large classrooms on the third floor to be used for Nursing Arts classes, I was involved in moving furniture to the third floor, as I have mentioned previously. Then Bronson purchased the school from the Kalamazoo Board of Education, and the print shop moved to the northeast corner of the third floor. I installed its new light fixtures and outlets. With Miss Noble in charge, purchasing also moved to the third floor, while the second floor contained the employee lounge and locker rooms. The large auditorium on the second floor was where Christmas parties, capping, senior breakfast and service award banquets took place. On the first floor, Edna Lord held her Public Health Clinic, which I'm sure all the student nurses remember. The library was also located on the south end of the first floor. The Harding gym was a great place for indoor sports. The Maintenance Department and my office were, for many years, in Harding's basement. Today, Harding has survived the wrecking ball, and new offices are presently being planned for this building. Oddly, it was the only building on Bronson property that Bronson did not have built.

Bronson was a great place to work. Our incredible group of retirees continues that fellowship each month. We're thankful for what the administration continues to do for us. Just as important, is that special friendship that has lasted all these years. To all the retirees and friends, once again I say, "Thank you," for your support and friendship.

Acknowledgements

Over the years, the employees in Human Resources (formerly, Personnel Department) at Bronson have been very helpful to me, not only in official business, but in other areas as well.

- Rick Geer who always saw that I was involved in events and programs in and out of the hospital
- Sue Copeland, for our monthly breakfasts and especially our retiree' picnic, particularly when they were held in the back of Truesdale Hall, and watched to see if the weather would cooperate
- Robin Welch at the retirees' breakfasts in many ways
- Priscilla Schau, we appreciated when our monthly breakfasts moved to the Senior Services building
- A special thanks to Julie and Nancy from dietary during the many years when our breakfasts were held in the Gilmore Center
- To all the retirees who came in an hour early to set up the breakfasts: Sue VandeGiessen, Arvid Erlandson, Bill Sootsman, Hazel Latondress, Barney Coville, Boop Vander Molen, Jack and Flo Wolthuis
- Bonnie Alkema, for getting speakers to our breakfast meetings in recent years
- Susan Walker with benefits and notification of retiree deaths
- Everyone in Human Resources for letting me sample all of the goodies in their department
- To all of the people I have inadvertently left out.

On three different occasions over the past 15 years, I have been presented with envelopes, cards and, on one occasion, a money tree from the retirees and my many friends, thanking me for publishing the retirees' newsletter and making arrangements for our monthly breakfasts and annual picnic. On the first occasion, I was presented with a money tree at our breakfast at Theo and Stacy's. The tree contained nearly $1,000. Naturally I was overwhelmed, as Smitty and Ralph Stewart said, "Now you and Boop can take a vacation." With our thanks and gratitude, we headed for Florida. Five years later, during our breakfast at the Gilmore Center, I was presented with an envelope. This time the money had grown to $1,840. With tears in my eyes I thanked everyone before heading off for another vacation. In another five years, Ellen Weston, handed me a large envelope with over $3,650, and said, "Thanks, Dick, from your many friends." I had all I could do to thank everyone and tell them it was nice to be appreciated by such great friends.

The final blow . . . On Wednesday, October 6, 2004, while doing volunteer duty at the hospital, I left my assigned area and walked down Lovell Street to watch the last of the hospital building that I really cared about being demolished. As I reflected back, I remembered the first to go were all the houses that the students had lived in, next Truesdale Hall, followed by Wesley Hall (the big dorm), the service building, the 1940 building, and then the ten-story hospital. Now, comes the final blow.

As I watched the first doctor's building in Kalamazoo, which housed our chapel, pharmacy, snack bar, business office and lobby, become a victim of time because Bronson could no longer find a use for any of it. I observed this once proud building being struck with the wrecking ball; I could almost feel the pain with each blow, reliving all of the memories it holds for me. It marked the end of an era of buildings that Dr. Perdew had built during his administration. Soon this area will be green space with bushes, flowers, etc. I know in years to come, as I will surely walk through it, my mind will wander back to those now long ago days, and remember the years when I called it my second home.

Epilogue

During my retirement, I have had a chance to reflect on my years at Bronson. I can't help but feel how fortunate I was to have been a part of the Bronson family. I say "family" because that's what we were back in the 40s, 50s and 60s.

Those were times when the patient was our number one concern . . . when we knew the doctors and called them by name . . . when student nurses wore caps, and you could tell freshmen from juniors and seniors . . . when we ate together in the cafeteria and talked over the events of the day, the Tigers and politics, etc. We laughed and maybe shed a few tears. We weren't concerned about such things as insurance reimbursement and government regulations, etc.

I know we didn't make much money nor have many benefits, but for some reason it didn't seem to matter that much.

We were a happy group of employees and student nurses, and could laugh and even play a few jokes. It was a time when the patients stayed in the hospital until they were well enough to go home, when we didn't have to lock all the hospital doors or hire security guards. We never gave a thought to or worried about layoffs, unions, Medicare forms, or a place to park your car.

The 70s came and went as we celebrated the 75th anniversary of the School of Nursing. The Pediatric/Adolescent building was dedicated. And then there was the blizzard of '78. We all thought, "Here we go again," when we were stranded at the hospital.

The 80s saw the retirement of President Daniel Finch. Also in the 80s you could call the hospital and talk to a person, not voice mail. The 1980s saw the first of many layoffs at the hospital, and it was hard for those of us who had to tell employees that their jobs had been eliminated. In 1986, we also saw the first early retirement plan implemented at Bronson, when, at the age of 56, I ended my employment at Bronson.

During the 90s many houses south of the old hospital, including the interns and residents buildings, were torn down. Pat Ludwig passed away unexpectedly and Frank Sardone replaced him as president and CEO of Bronson Healthcare Group. Ground was broken for the *New* Bronson.

In the year 2000, we saw the *New* Bronson open and celebrate 100 years of Bronson Methodist Hospital service to the Kalamazoo community. We watched the demolition of Wesley Hall, the 1940 Building, the ten-story main hospital and the Medical West Building.

The Vander Molen Heritage

The Vander Molen family was well represented at Bronson Methodist Hospital over the years. I worked for 41 years at Bronson. Boop spent her years at Bronson in Peds and Obstetrics/Deliveries. Craig worked as a security guard while completing his master's degree at Western Michigan University. Steve started his employment at Bronson while going to Western, and now has completed 27 years there. Cheri never worked at the hospital, but did pitch for the first Bronson women's softball team. She did, however, choose dental hygiene as her profession. My brother, Andy, and his wife Donna, were both employed by Bronson for several years. My sister, Esther, worked in Central Supply for many years as well. This family history shows that Bronson was a great place to work, especially for the Vander Molens.

Throughout this book, I have not tried to tell you about the medical advances or expanded services during my years at Bronson, of which I am very proud. Instead I have tried to tell you about the people who came together to serve the sick in a special way during a period of great growth and expansion.

I also want you to know that we employees could take time away from work to enjoy the friendship of those with whom we worked, whether it was from Bronson-sponsored softball, basketball or bowling teams, or just meeting for coffee. This is what made Bronson employees very special. We were a close knit group who felt we were needed, appreciated and part of a team serving the patients.

Today the friendship continues as 100 retirees meet every month at the Kalamazoo Senior Services building for breakfast and a program to reminisce about our days at Bronson. Just as I have looked back, let us also look forward to exciting times as we continue the healing ministry of Christ to the sick whom we will serve in the 2000s.

~

The Bronson I Knew

INDEX

Boldface page numbers indicate **photographs**.

A

Accidents, 31–32, 91, 123
Adams, Lou, 121
Adams, Miss, 5, 21
Adkins, Esther, 157
Affiliations, 21, 45, 48, 126
    pediatric, 28, 78, 94
    rural public health, 93
    state hospital, 78, 95
Alcoholic drinks, 39, 83, 105, 131, 164
Alexander, George, 167, 171
Alkema, Bonnie, 236
Ambulance services, 22, 67, **87**
American Society for Hospital Engineering, 219
Anderson, Miss Mary B. ("Mary B."), 49
    accidents reported to, 32, 123
    administrative roles of, 8–9, 11, 102, 157, 159

Anderson, Miss Mary B. ("Mary B."), *cont.*
    attendance at parties and outings, 80–81, 131, 133
    BMH nursing school anniversary and, 209
    communication through, 57, 63, 76, 94, 108–109
    resignation of, 161–162, 167
    smoking and, 31, 162
    student nurses' dorm and, 23, 124, 126
    working for, 13, 23–24, 28–29, 40, 66, 82, 92, 132, 137–138
Anderson Hall, 163–164, 185
Animal care, 1, 3–10, 53
    Guild House basement, 4–6, 7–8
Annex, The, 43, 49

Appel and Appel, medical center offices, 91
Ashby, Debbie, 64
Ashby, Junior, 63–64, 167–168
Assassinations, 170
Attics, 48, 59, 83
Austin Lake, trips to, 72
Automobiles
 borrowing, 65
 owning, 71, 115
 parking areas for, 22, **87**, 186–187
 trips in, 65–66, 72, 154, 221, 222

B
Baas, John, 220
[Backert?], Mr. See Herman (kitchen staff)
Baird, Mrs. ("Mother"), 106, 128, 154, 186
Balkema family, 1
Banker, Reva, 30
Barnett, Chuck, 204
Baseball games, 2, 112, 116, 168. See also Detroit Tigers (baseball)
Basketball games, 19, 132, 156, 162, 169
 practice facilities, 134, 200
Beard, Nancy, 46
Beatty, Mrs. Martha, 73–74, 117, 125

Beatty, Mrs. Martha, *cont.*
 Boop dating Dick and, 75–77
Beck, Herb, **195,** 212, 227
Behnke, Marilyn, 129
Bellis, Bob, 224
Bennett and Bennett. medical center offices, 91
Best, Earnest, **193**, 227–228
Betz and DePree, medical center offices, 91
BHG. See Bronson Healthcare Group
Big sisters, 48
Black-banding, 65
Blanche (seamstress), 59
BMH. *See* Bronson Methodist Hospital
Book crates, 30
Boop. *See* Gosling, Betty Lou ("Boop"); Vander Molen, Richard ("Dick") and Betty ("Boop")
Boshoven, Howard, 223
Bouserman, Bob, 224
Bowers, John, 77, 109, 110
Boyhood friends, 2–3, 10, 23, 26
Bronson, Titus, 74
Bronson Healthcare Group, 212, 213, 227, 228–229, 240

Index

Bronson Methodist Hospital
  anniversaries, 197, 205, 233, 240
  dedications at, 99, 103, 212
  families employed by, 63–64, 208, 211, 238, 240
  gifts to student nurses by, 96, 122, 230
  huge oaks on front lawn, 74–75
  logo change, 207
  money matters and, 25, 33, 44, 237 (see also Fundraising)
  motto, 111, 148
  national awards to, 228
  the New Bronson (*see* New Bronson Methodist Hospital, The)
  reflections on being employed by, 19–20, 37, 47–49, 80, 92, 114, 137, 148, 232, 235, 238–240
Bronson Methodist Hospital, board, 41
  administrators appointed by, 123–124, 159
  properties purchased by, 45, 119, 122, 134, 164, 234
Bronson Methodist Hospital, committees
  Christmas, 171
  Energy, 206, 210
  special, 226
Bronson Methodist Hospital, employees, 35
  distribution of
    administration, 22, 103, 118, 159, 160, 178, 185, 199–200, 201
    animal care, 6, 10, 23
    carpenters, 18, 56, 172
    central supply, 159, 240
    chaplain, 117
    dieticians, 58, 95, 113
    electricians, 56, 104, 172
    engineers, 18, 137, 183, 184–185
    firemen, 25, 61, 62, 63, 164, 172
    housekeeping, 62, 66, 186
    human resources department, 235

245

Bronson Methodist
Hospital,
employees,
distribution of, *cont.*
kitchen, 22, 63–64,
65, **89**
laboratory, 6–7,
21, 107, 159
laundry, 59, 62,
177–178, 228
maintenance crew
(*see under*
Bronson's
Maintenance
Department,
crew in)
mechanics, 56,
114, 172, 181,
208
orderlies, 174, 186
painters, 4, 7, 25,
158, 172
personnel
department,
133, 178, 200,
214
purchasing agents,
65, 206
x-ray department,
19
early retirement plan
for, 214, 238
as fund contributors,
94, 113, 122, 171,
205

Bronson Methodist
Hospital,
employees, *cont*
housing for, 8, 23, 43,
49, 56, **87**, 163–
164, 188, 228
job layoffs and losses
for, 226, 239
numbers of, 62, 133,
190, 206
team spirit among, 59,
60, 202, 240-241
Bronson Methodist
Hospital,
expansion, 64, 103
construction begins,
67–68, 133, 175,
201
construction continues,
73, 78, 80, 92, 96,
97, 181, 202, 231
demolition for, 185,
196, 201, 213, 216,
228, 237–238, 239
fundraising for, 94, 99,
119, 122–123, 171,
188
remodeling, 100, 131,
153, 198–199, 205–
206, 211–212
Bronson Methodist
Hospital, facilities,
132, 236–237
administration
auditorium, 3, 18,
27–28, 35, 95,
137

246

Bronson Methodist Hospital, facilities, administration, *cont.*
    entrances, 21–22, 67, **87,** 91, 126, 201, 213
    lobby, 225
    offices, 91, 172
food service
    baby formula room, 113
    bakery, 103, 205
    cafeteria, 22, 103, 104–105, 125, 135, 199, 201
    diet kitchen, 37, 198
    fruit cellar, 24–25
    garden area, 67
    snack bar, 91, 103–104, 147, 176, 190, 199
infrastructure
    boiler room, 25, 61
    central supply, 37, 100, 111–112, 147–148
    chapel, 75, 91–92, 98–99
    classrooms, 67
    data processing, 188
    Gilmore Center, 212, 216, 233, 236
    heating plant, 100

Bronson Methodist Hospital, facilities, infrastructure, *cont,*
    helicopter landing pad, 212
    housekeeping, 67, 112
    laboratories, 3, 43, 58, 100, 181
    laundry, 17, 22, 58–59, 67, 181, 227
    libraries, 235
    maintenance sheds and shops, 56–57, 63, **87** (*see also* Bronson's Maintenance Department)
    morgue, 22
    pharmacy, 91–92, 112, 200
    physical facilities department (*see old name*, Bronson's Maintenance Department)
    power plant, 172, 175
    tunnel, 127, 128, 159, 232
    x-ray department, 25, 58, 100, 197

Bronson Methodist
  Hospital, facilities,
  cont.
  patient areas
    children's
      playroom, 68
    clinics, 171, 235
    emergency room,
      22, 32, 61, 67,
      73, 100, 125,
      147, 211
    hemodialysis unit,
      189
    outpatient surgery,
      212
    pediatrics, 58
    physical therapy,
      100
    surgery, 57, 100,
      105, 123, 147,
      201, 204
    wards, 37, 57, 78,
      206
Bronson Methodist
  Hospital, floors
  2 East, 130, 201, 226
  Hall 1, 13, 58, 78
  Hall 3, 153
  Hall 4, 211
  Hall 5, 57, 84–85, 98,
    187
  Hall 6, 65, 98, 101,
    112, 153, 187, 211,
    219
  Hall 8, 205–206
  Hall 9, 205–206

Bronson Methodist
  Hospital, floors,
  cont.
  OB/Deliveries, 16, 57,
    133, 157, 169–170,
    203, 239
  OR/Surgeries, 169–
    170
  1 West, 33
  2 West, 16, 32, 58, 206
Bronson Methodist
  Hospital, patients,
  24–25
  care of, 80, 98, 148,
    178–180, 237, 240–
    241
  Dick as one of, 31–33,
    78, 189, 219
  Donny Fee, 178–180
  Grandma Hale as, 130,
    22–227
  Ralph Stewart, 228
Bronson Methodist
  Hospital School of
  Nursing, 119, 127
  "Alma Mater," 118,
    126, 230
  alumnae/alumni
    activities, 122, 207,
      217–218, 224-226,
      230
  anniversaries, 117,
    209, 239
  classrooms for, 60, 67,
    73
  directors, 161, 165,
    166, 207

Bronson Methodist
Hospital School of
Nursing, *cont.*
enrollment numbers,
50, 92, 133, 166,
201
excellent training in,
98, 117, 231
reflections on whole
experience of, 128–
129, 218
social director for, 73–
74, 117
Bronson Park,
Kalamazoo, 96, 221
*Bronson Retirees'
Newsletter,* 220,
228
Bronson's Maintenance
Department, 82,
151, 175, 184, 201
cafeteria and snack
bar camaraderie
within, 22, 25, 56,
104–105, 114, 159
crew in, 58, 62, **87,**
119, 136, **152,** 183,
184, 202, 207, 215
department heads, 18,
137, 177, 181–182,
184, 203–205
facilities move of, 67,
73, 81
jobs done by
emergencies, 112,
121, 126, 181,
182, 206

Bronson's Maintenance
Department,
jobs done by, *cont.*
food events, 202–
203, 205
homecoming
floats, 103
ice-carving
assistance, 167
moving equipment
and furniture,
126–127, 204,
233
remodeling, 198
supplying
equipment,
230–231
wiring for
Hollywood film,
169–170
opinions of guys in, 41,
97
preventive
maintenance
program in, 187–
188, 203
as section, 171–172,
189, 212
Brown, Betty, 36
Brown, Mrs. Louise, 165
Brush, Bill, 72, 82, 98,
184
as Bronson employee,
52, 62, 66–67, 68
gab sessions with, 61,
69, 70, 77, **89**
Bryant, Mr., 154

Bulletin, The (newsletter), BMH School of Nursing alumni, 225
Burns, Al, 106
Burton Heights Methodist Church, Grand Rapids, 109, 110
Bushouse, Nelson, **192**

C

Cadet nurses, 21, 48, 69
Cafeteria, 24–25. *See also under* Bronson Methodist Hospital, facilities, food service, cafeteria
Call systems, 59, 78, 153, 155–156
Capping, 35, 46, 48, 126, 235
Card games, 2, 176–177
Carpenters, 18, 56, 172
Cars. *See* Automobiles
Catalyst, The (newspaper), 167–168, 197
Cedar Home, 107, 163
 housemothers, 79, 102, 117
 replaced by new dorm, 119–120, 124
Children's Hospital, Detroit, 28
Chocolate Shop, gifts from, 73
Choirs, student nurses' in, 99, 103

Christian, Mr. O.K., 3
Christian Endeavor, 198, 221–222
Christmastime festivities, 62, 122, 165, 171
 formal dances, 34, 131, **191**
 maintenance crew and, **152**, 203
 meals during, 45–46, 72–73
 parties on the 6th floor, 73, 80–81, 118
 tree decoration, 45–46, 130
Church, Mrs., 93
Cigarettes, 31, **89**, 162, 197
Civil Defense radio, 208
Claflin, Connie, 30
Clark, Dorothy (cashier), 159, 167
Clark, Jackie. See Wylie, Jackie Clark
Clark, Maxine Ketchum, 63, 211
Coca-Cola, deliveries, 20
Coleman, Miss, 17
Comstock, Thelma, 2
Comstock, Vic, 2
Conklin, Mrs., 17, 40
Conrad and Hanson, medical center offices, 91
Conscientious objectors (I-W), 129, 156, 226
Copeland, Sue, 236

Index

Coville, Barney, 236
Crosstown Center, 212
Curtis, Don, 107
Cutright, Linda, 168

D
Daleiden's Auto Shop, 1
Dances, 34, 48, 100, 125, 128, 131
Dating
    Boop and Dick, 75–77, 93, 94–95
    double, 68, 77, 95, 107
    nursing students, 73–74, 77, 84
Degoffau, Joan, **191**
Deliverymen, 19, 20
Derby Inn, 79
Detroit, Michigan, affiliations, 28
Detroit Tigers (baseball)
    attending, games, 72, 107–109, 168–169, 209
    fans, 22, 64–65, 111, 125, 179
    listening to, games on radio, 69, 111
    predictions about, 112, 160–161
Dillon, Louise, 165
Doctors, 33, 37, 80
    dining rooms for, 22, 104–105, 199
    dinner dance for nurses, 48, 100

Doctors, *cont.*
    interns, 98, 111, 120, 177, 188, 201, 229
    offices for, 91, 185, 200, 231
    parking area for, 22, **87**
    residents, 98, 111, 120, 163–164, 172, 177, 188, 229
Doctors remembered A–H
    Ajemian, 202
    Andrews, 185
    Appel, 91
    Bennett, 91
    Betz, 91, 116
    Birch, 91, 115
    Boys, 33
    Camp, 120
    Conrad, 91
    DePree, 91, 116, 147, 166
    Dew, 91, 113
    Dvorak, 163–164
    Fast, 148
    Finton, 91
    Friend, 120
    Fry, 120
    Gerstner, 33
    Hanson, 91
    Heersma, 91, 234
    Herbert, 65, 111, 116, 147
    Hoebeke, 91
    Hubbel, 91

Doctors remembered, *cont.*
  J–Z
    Jackson, 32, 33, 116
    Jennings, 33
    Kaufman, 120
    Kilgore, 91, 104, 116, 176
    King, 111
    Lavender, 91
    Lubavs, 111
    Machin, 49
    Marshall, 91
    Martens, 91
    May, 75, 111, 234
    Patmos, 91, 120–121
    Patow, 75, 98
    Peelen, 91
    Proos, 120
    Robinson, 49, 65
    Scholten, 91
    Schrier, 91
    Springgate, 156, 223
    VanderVelde, 91
    Weadon, 147
    Wiley, 120
    Wilson, **150**, 166
    Zimont, 120
    See also Prentice, Dr. Hazel; Perdew, Dr. William

Dorms aka "homes away from home." *See specifics, i.e.,*
  Anderson Hall;
  Annex, The;
  Cedar Home;
  East Home;
  North Home;
  Pine Home;
  South Home;
  Truesdale Hall;
  Wesley Hall
Drake, Janet, 120
Duflo, Dale, 208-209
  awards, **191**, 203
  maintenance crewman, **152**, 158, 160, 182, 198
Dutch Market, 148
Dutch origins, 97, 148, 209

E
Eash, Amos, 59
East Home, 44, 50, 70, 79, 216
  housemothers, 45
East Medical Center, 232
Edgerton, Marge, 21
Edison Elementary School, 47
Eigsti, Clarence, **192**
Eisenhower, Gen. Dwight D., 61, 158
Electricians, 25, 56, 104, 172

Electrocardiography laboratory, 43
Elevators
  in Truesdale Hall, 127
  in Wesley Hall, 13–15, 20, 30, 48, 114
Elley, Frank, 185
Ellis, Mrs. ("Mother"), 45, **90**, 153, 154
  in Cedar Home, 102
  in North Home, 40, 41, 44, 52, 59
  in Pine Home, 79, 83, 84, 96, 97
Elmore, Miss, 7
Emaar twins, 2
Employee Service Awards, 164, 174, 176–177, 189–190, **195,** 203, 211
  banquets for, 234
Engineers
  organizations of, 205, 219
  Plant Operations with, 171–172, 212
  seminars for, 183–184, 209
  See also Lamothe, Omer; Rothwell, Floyd
Engle, Ginnie, 124
Erlandson, Arvid, 236
Evans, Shirley, 35, 58
Evelyn (kitchen staff), 65
Extension cords, 70–71, 79–80

F
Fee, Donny, 178–180
Fetters, Shirley, 125
"51" (newspaper), 93
Filler, John, 202
Finch, Mr. Daniel N., 159–160, 171, 177, **193**
  appointments by, 164–165, 166
  Bronson Healthcare Group and, 213, 239
  employee service awards from, 174, 203, 211
  as hospital spokesman, 181, 182, 199
  staffing changes under, 161–162, 167, 184–185, 209
Firemen, 61, 62
  Bill Wiggins, 25
  George Todd, 75
  Howard the moviemaker, 80
  Jim Pearson, 63
First Methodist Church, Kalamazoo, 48
  nurses' graduation at, 28, 41, 50, 101–102, 124, 136, 166, 230
First Reformed Church, Kalamazoo, 61
  guys from, in Naval Reserve, 77, 98

First Reformed Church, Kalamazoo, *cont.*
   sports teams from, 19, 209
   Vander Molen activities and membership in, 198, 221–223
Fish fry, 203
Fishing, 75, 82, 202
Fitzpatrick, Sam, **192**
Flower, Mrs. Ethel, 95
Food supplies, 132
   canned, 24–25, 44
   delivered to kitchens, 29, 43, 49, 93, 97
   "goodies" as, 35, 44, 62, 73, 128, 148
   janitor's orientation about, 16–17
Ford, Gerald R., 188
Fortune, Karl, **192**
Fred (maintenance crewman), **152**
Froyd, Peter, 185, 189, 213, 216, 226
Fruit cellars, 164
Fruit jars, 44
Fundraising
   building funds, 94, 171
   dormitory for student nurses, 119, 122–123
   Kindleberger chapel, 98–99
   United Way, 205
Funk, Barb, 106

F.W. Woolworth Company, 210

G

Geer, Rick, 178, 182, 214, 220, 236
Genevieve U. and Donald S. Gilmore Center for Health Education, 212, 216, 233, 236
Gibson, Mr. Karl
   as boss, 85, 228
   offices of, 10–11, 80, 156, 158–159, 176
Gift-giving
   donations
      corporate, 188, 231
      employee, 94, 171, 180, 206
      private, 212
      School of Nursing alumnae, 122
      White Cross Guild, 24–25, 98–99, 122
   personal, 208, 215–216, 217–218, 237
   winter holidays and, 73, 96, 122
Gilbert, Mrs. Marjorie, 165, 171
Gilmore's department store, 212
Golf outings, 223–224

Index

Gosling, Betty Lou ("Boop"), **149, 151**
    car trips while single, 66, 83–84, 97, 108
    dating, 75–77, 93, 94–95
    family, 83–84, 94, 95, 97, 101–102, 107, 109
    graduation, 101–102, **151**
    roommates of, 69, 71, 76, 94, 102, 106, 109
    See also Vander Molen, Richard ("Dick") and Betty ("Boop")
Gosling, Shirley, 83, 109
Gould, Barb, 112, 113
Gould, Margaret, 46
Grace (cafeteria cashier), 22
Graduation ceremonies, 201
    diplomas and pins, 28, 102, 127, 162, 166
    KCHS, and Dick, 46–47
    nurses', at First Methodist, 28, 41, 50, 101–102, 124, 136, 166, 230
Graduation pictures, KCHS, 46, **89**
Graham, Hugh, 204
Grauman, Wanda, 19, 46
Groat, Mrs. Thelma, 35, 147–148, 159
Grote, Judy, 129
Guild House. See under White Cross Guild
Gurd, Ray, 189, 201, 206
Gurgenson, Roger, **192**

H

Haas, Sue, 220
Haines, Mrs., 19, 25, 30, 40
Hale, Mrs. ("Grandma"), 130, 226–227
Hall, G. Ray, ambulance service of, 22, 67, 73, **87,** 126
Hamamura, Tomo, 65–66
Hamburgers, 79, 83, 157
Harding Auditorium
    Christmas parties in, 171, **192,** 235
    other activities in, 148, 168, 182, 190, 198
Harding School building, 35, 177
    gym in, 134, 182, 199–200, 234–235
    new facilities near, 175, 181
    rented classrooms in, 60, 234
    as survivor, 232, 235
Hauke, Pat, 114
Health education building, 212
Healthcare Plaza, 212

Hecht, Elaine, 21
Hecker, Louie, 224
Heersma, Dr. Sid, 91, 234
Heersma and Dew,
 medical center
 offices, 91
Helicopters, 212
Hell Week, 36, 48
Herb medicine lesson, 64
Herbert, Dr., 65, 111, 116, 147
Herman (kitchen staff), 16–17, 24–25, **89**
Heydenberk, Jerry, 176–177
Heystek, Herman, 19, 58
Hoebeke and Birch,
 medical center
 offices, 91
Hoffman, Jim, 203, 206, 210
Holben, Sue, **191**
Holcome, Mrs., 92
Holidays, working on, 56, 61
Homesickness, 48
Hospital physical facilities. *See old name,* Bronson's Maintenance Department
Houghland, David and Debbie, **194,** 234
Houghland grandchildren, **194,** 234
House directors
 Mrs. Gilbert, 147

House directors, *cont.*
 Mrs. Lewis, 129, 147
Housekeepers, 22, 80, 130
 Amos Eash, 59
 Mrs. Holcome, 92
 Mrs. Irwin, 92
 Mrs. Richardson, 24, 47, 92
 Mrs. Rinehart, 24, 47, 92
 Mrs. Roe, 19, 25
 retirements of, 92, 102, 186
 wall-washers as, 66
 See also Smith, Ruby
Housemothers, **90,** 128–129
 Miss Coleman, 17, 40
 Mrs. Conklin, 17, 40
 Mrs. Irwin, 92
 Mrs. Ketchum, 112
 Mrs. Lyons, 117–118, 121
 Mrs. Synwolt, 117–118
 Mrs. Wotring, 117, 154
 See also Ellis, Mrs. ("Mother"); Howell, Mrs.; Kirk, Mrs.; Reusch, Mrs.; Wright, Mrs. ("Granny")
Howard (moviemaker), 80
Howell, Mrs., **90**
 loss of, 49, 154
 in South Home, 40, 44, 46

Index

Hubbel and Kilgore,
  medical center
  offices, 91
Huckendubler, Ken, 200,
  205, 212, 214
Huffman, Miss, 126

I
I-W boys. *See*
  Conscientious
  objectors
Ice skating, 3
Ice supplies, 14, 16–17,
  24, 29, 167
Identification devices, 93,
  182–183
Ironsides, Mrs., 154
Irwin, Mrs. Harriet, 92

J
Jackson, Dr. Howard, 32,
  33, 116
Jacob Kindleberger
  Memorial Chapel,
  75, 98–99
Jake (garbageman), 57
Jerry (lab tech), 159
Jeske, Marie. *See*
  McLeieer, Marie
  Jeske
John (boyhood neighbor),
  2, 10, 23
Johnson, W.E., 184, 200
Johnson, William A., 213
Joldersma and Klein
  Funeral Home, 79
Junior bands, 36

K
Kalamazoo, downtown
  churches, 222
  hotels, 186, 212–213,
    230
  movie theatres, 79,
    157
  the New Bronson and,
    228
  parks, 96, 221
  restaurants, 39, 79, 95,
    157
  retail areas, 95, 210,
    212
Kalamazoo Central High
  School, 1, 3
  Dick's senior year, 39,
    41–42, 46
  education at, vs.
    Wesley Hall, 19, 43
  graduation from, 47, **89**
Kalamazoo College,
  dating guys from,
  73–74, 75–76
Kalamazoo County, Parks
  and Recreation
  Commission, 189
Kalamazoo Gazette
  (newspaper), 231–
  232
Kalamazoo Ice and Fuel
  Co., 1
Kalamazoo Mall, 95
Kalamazoo parks
  Bronson, 96, 221
  Crosstown ponds, 3

257

Kalamazoo parks, *cont.*
  Milham, 82–83, **149,** 221
  Upjohn, 1, 2–3, 68
Kalamazoo Public Schools, 47, 134, 156. *See also specifics, e.g.,* Harding School
Kalamazoo restaurants
  the Birches, 215
  Colonial Kitchen, 223
  Derby Inn, 79
  Holly's, 157, 213
  Home Restaurant, 39
  Matthew's, 46
  Schensul's, 95
  Theo & Stacey's, **193,** 237
Kalamazoo State Hospital, 37, 78–79, 95
Kalamazoo streets
  Academy, 221
  Burdick, 26, 31, 95, 100, 210, 229
  Carr, 1, 2, 6, 68, **86,** 110
  Cedar, 22, 23, 45, 127, 185
  Church, 221
  Crosstown Parkway, 3
  Drake, 223
  Dutton, 201
  Henrietta, 79

Kalamazoo streets, *cont.*
  Jasper, 35, 164, 172, 201
  John, 115
    dorms on, 17, 23, 36, 44, 49, 163
    hospital-purchased houses on, 164, 172
    the *New* Bronson on, **196,** 213
    staff housing constructed on, 188
  Kook, 164
  Lake, 1, 2, 77
  Lovell, 45
    businesses near, 79, 95
    Harding School on corner, 35
    hospital entrance on, 3, 103, 213, 225
    North Home on, 17, 36, 44, 79
    parking areas, 156, 158, 201
  Pine, 79, 127, 212
    dorms on, 79
    hospital-purchased properties on, 45, 119, 122, 126, 164
    name change, 212
    traffic jam on, 127
  Portage, 1, 2

Index

Kalamazoo streets, *cont.*
  South, 95
  Stadium, 223
  Vine, 1, 2, 115, 164
  Walnut, 164
  Westnedge, 229
Kalamazoo Vegetable Parchment Company, 99
KCHS. *See* Kalamazoo Central High School
Kennedy, Bobby, 170
Kennedy, Pres. John F., 169–170
Kesselring, Margie, 106
Ketchum, Karyle, 63, 211
Ketchum, Mrs., 63, 112, 154
Kettenbiel, Dan, 204
Kiewet, Joan, 73
Kilgore, Dr., 91, 104, 116, 176
King, Martin Luther, Jr., 170
Kirk, Mrs., 30, 31, 154, **191**
  Dick treated as son of, 14, 16, 26, 39–40
  janitor's orientation from, 13–16, 18, 28, 29
  job in New Mexico, 40, 47
Kirk, Richard, 13, **191**
Kleis, Paul, 223
Klose Electric Company, 115
Klute, Miss Helen, 113, 167
Kneen, Russell P., 213, 216, 227
Korendyke, Ben, 182
Kostakis, Jim, 208
Krieger, Joyce, 121
Kruger, John, 136, 160–161, 176, 199

L

Lamothe, Omer, 184
  chief engineer, 137, 158, 183, 205
  respect for, 158, 182
Lampos, Mike, 178, 187
Landmarks, front lawn, 74–75, 99
LaRoy, Lou, 107
Larva, Laddie, 103
Latondress, Hazel ("Smitty"), 165
  awards given and received, 211, 236
  as nursing director, 165, 199, 206
  as volunteer, 220, 236-237
Lechner, Paul, **152**, 175, 200
Lecos, Gus, 167, 171, 178, 187
LeCronier, Phyl, 107
Lee, Everine, 157
Leflore, Charlie, **192**
Lehman, Harvey, **192**
Leonard, Nancy, 236

259

Lewis, Happy, 52
Lewis, Mrs. Clara, 129, 147
Long Lake, trips to, 68, 72, 221
Long-term care facility, 122
Lord, Edna, 235
Lott, Mr. S.A., 73
Ludwig, Patric ("Pat"), 227, 228, 239
Lyons, Mrs. ("Mother"), 117–118, 121, 154

M

Mac (yardman), 57
MacDougal sisters, 168–169
Maids. See Housekeepers
Mail carriers, 19
Mailboxes, 128
Man bell
    button for, 13–14, 52–53
    warning from, 20, 29, 69, 118
Marcus (electrician), 56
Married student policy, 126
Marshall, Michigan, affiliations, 93, 94, 95
Marshall and Finton, medical center offices, 91

Martens and Lavender, medical center offices, 91
Martha (formula room employee), 113
Martin, Marty, as Mrs. Bowers, 109
Martin, Sharon, 133–134
Martin, Shirley, 114
Mary B. See Anderson, Miss Mary B. ("Mary B.")
Mason, Miss Mary, 167, 171
Maxwell, Mrs., 33, 58
May, Dr. Donald, 75, 111, 234
Mayberry, Michigan, affiliations, 28
Mayfield, Jane, 19, 46
McLeieer, Marie Jeske, 114, 225
McLeod, Kathryn, **191**
McNally, Joan, 106
McPhail, Miss Virginia ("Ginny"), 30, 73, 164–165
MDOL. See Michigan Department of Labor
Medical centers, 78, 91, 104, 201, 232, 240
Melson, Miss, 40
Memorial chapel. See Jacob Kindleberger Memorial Chapel
Meninga, Dorothy, **192**

Index

Mercer, Peggy, 136
Messer, Bristol ("Brit"), 200
Methodists, 24–25, 44–45, 158–159
   churches (*see* Burton Heights Methodist Church, Grand Rapids; First Methodist Church, Kalamazoo)
Meyer, Ralph, 167, **192**
Meyers, Harvey, 19, 58–59, 177, 228
Meyle, Mrs. Mabel Stell. *See under* Stell, Mrs. Mabel
Michigan, healthcare regulation, 37, 93
Michigan Department of Labor (MDOL), unions and, 198
Mickey, Bob, 223
Milham Park, picnics at, 82–83, **149**, 221
Military service
   conscientious objectors to, 129, 156, 226
   Dick and friends in, 77, 98, **149**
Miller, Floyd, **192**
Miller, Mrs., 32
Miller-Davis Company, 182
Moerman, Kit, 2
Moffat, Miss, R.N., 18, 48

Morgan, Helen, 33
Motyer, Derwin, 66, 147
Motyer, Gwen, 65–66
Motyer, Shirley, 65–66
Mount Clemens, Michigan, affiliations, 78, 94, 95
Movies, 80–81
   dating and, 61, 68, 95
   downtown Kalamazoo, 79, 157
Mrs. Gilbert, 147
Murray, Sue. *See* VandeGeisen, Sue Murray
Musselman, Ted, 204
Mutt and Jeff, 114, 153

N
Naniga, Henry, 3
Nap, Dick, 223
Nedervelt, Martha, 126
Neiley, Bill, **192**
Nelson, Clara, 115
Nelson boys, military service of, 98
New Bronson Methodist Hospital, The, 213, 232
   facilities in, 220, 231
   ground breaking for, 229, 240
   volunteers in retirement at, **196,** 220–221, 224, 231

Newsletters, 220, 225, 228
Newspapers, 93, 167–168, 197, 231–232
Nicknames, 48. See also Vander Molen, Richard ("Dick"), nicknames
Nixon, Richard M., campaign, 188, 189
Noble, Miss, 65, 234
North Home, 24, 37, 216
 attic in, 59, 83
 front porch on, 26–27, 36, 44–45
 housemothers at, 17, 40, 41, 43–44, 50, 79
 juniors move to, 21, 41
 kitchen supplies for, 14, 16–17, 43
 layout of, 45, 79
 location of, 79, 122
Nottingham, Lyle, 35, 57, 123, 174, 209
Nurses, 93, 103, 205
 caps of (see Blackbanding; Capping)
 dances for, 48, 100, 125
 Dick dates, 73–74
 Dick learns names of, 19, 41, 50, 79, 130
 Dick meets, 25, 29, 31–32, 42–43, 45, 69–71, 72, 107, 198

Nurses, *cont.*
 education and training (*see under* Affiliations; Michigan; Nursing schools)
 Hell Week for, 36, 48
 impressions of, 18, 21, 121
 move into new dorm, 127–128
 traditions for, 69, 120
Nurses' aides, 68, 84–85, 126
Nurses remembered
 1940s' classes
 '45, 21
 '46, 41
 '47, 45, 50, 154
 '48, 28–30, 34, 45, 50, 69
 '49, 39, 41, 46, 50, 78–79
 1950s' classes
 '50, 50, 51, 69–70
 '51, 69, 70, 93, 101–102
 '52, 79–80, 102, 107, 112
 '53, 92–93, 97, 102, 112, 117, 119
 '54, 102, 106, 113, 115, 117
 '55, 112, 114, 119, 120
 '56, 117, 121–122

262

Index

Nurses remembered,
1950's classes, *cont.*
'57, 118, 122, 126, 127
'58, 120, 125, 126, 127, 133, 134
'59, 125, 126, 127, 134, 135–136
1960s' classes
'60, 128, 137, 156
'61, 133, 162
'62, 137, 166
'63, 156, 169
'64, 165
1970s' classes
'72, 201
1990s' classes
'98, 229
Nursing schools. *See* Bronson Methodist Hospital School of Nursing; *and under* Western Michigan University, Bronson School of Nursing

O

Oak trees (landmarks), 74–75, 99
Oaklawn Hospital, Marshall, 93
Open houses, 127, 185, 197

P

Painters, 7, 25, 158, 172
Parchment, Michigan, residence in, 123, 125
Parking areas, 172, 233
doctors' cars, 22, **87**
ramps, 201, 229
visitors' cars, 156, 158, 213
Parties, 48, 188, 232
alumnae/alumni, 217, 229–230
Christmastime, 62, 73, 118, 203, 235
farewell, for bosses, 183, 184, 215
retirement, 215–217
student nurses', 35, 36, 128, 134, 156
Patmos, Dr. Martin, medical center offices, 91, 120–121
Patow, Dr. Warren, 75, 98
Pearson, Jim, 63
Pediatric-Adolescent building, 185, 197, 203, 229, 233, 239
Pediatrics ("Peds"), 57, 126, 178–180, 239
Peelen and VanderVelde, medical center offices, 91
Peg-Leg Louie (kitchen staff), 64
Perdew, Dr. William, 44, 62–63, 80

263

Perdew, Dr. William, *cont.*
  attendance at parties and outings, 80–81, 108, 131
  death and memories of, 158, 226, 229
  dreams of, 127, 238
  graduation duties of, 50, 102
  speeches by, 27–28, 73, 127, 137
  supervision by, 104, 123–124, 132, 157, 159
Perdew, Mrs. Mary H., 130, 158, 226–227
Personnel policies, 126, 137, 166
Peters, Miss, 148
Peterson, Nancy, 129
Philippine nurses, 206
Picnics
  in Milham Park, 82–83, **149**, 221
  in Truesdale's backyard, 128, 226, 236
Pidgley, Mrs. Hilda, 147, 171, 176, **192**
Pine Auditorium, 119, 126
Pine Home, 79, 97, 163, 216
  housemothers, 83, 102, 122
  recreation room TV in, 96, 107, 116

Pine Home, *cont.*
  replaced by new dorm, 119–120, 124
Pinkster, Jerry, 182
Pneumatic tube system, 111–112
Polio ward, 78, 113
Politics, 125, 176
  county, 189
  national, 158, 188–189
  predictions about, 160–161
  state, 177
Ponejolic, Jean, 215
Pontiac coupe, 71
Potter, Forrest, 4, 7, 25, 58, 73, 81
Powell, Ken, 181, 204, 215
Practical nurses, 163
Pratt, Mr. John C., 118, 158, 159, 164
"Prayer for peace," 27–28
Pregnancy tests, 7, 11
Prentice, Dr. Hazel, 58, 81
  job interview with, 3–5
  John and, 11, 23
  working for, 5–10, 53
Proxmire, Mary, 47
Public health, 93, 183–184, 235

R
Radio operators, 208
Radio programs, 2, 26, 69, 111

Radiology facilities. *See under* Bronson Methodist Hospital, facilities, infrastructure, x-ray department
Railroad tracks, 2, 125
Ramer, Junior, 3
Ramps (parking), 200, 228
Ramps (pedestrian), 91
Rasmussen, Jennie, 107
Rathburn, Van and Terry, 233
Rathburn grandchildren, **194,** 233
Reagan, Ronald, 188
Recreation activities
  administrative support for, 118, 241
  indoors, 2, 19, 45, 134–135, 176
  instrumental and vocal music as, 130, 132, 134, 156, 169, 212
  outdoors, 2, 3, 45, 82–83, 138, 158, 177, 223–224
  See also specifics, *e.g.,* Basketball games; Golf outings; Softball games; Tennis
Reed, Sally, 157
Refrigerators, in dorms, 24

Reimer, Ada, 80–81, 82–83
Republican National Convention, 188
Resh, Judy, 129
Retirees' media, 197, 220, 228
Retirements
  administrators, 176, 177, 200, 209, 213, 216
  food service, 176
  housekeepers, 92, 102, 186
  housemothers, 92, 154
  lab technicians, 102, 176–177
  maintenance crew, 158, 176, **196,** 202, 204, 208
  nurses, 166–167, 187, **196,** 207
Reusch, Mrs., **90,** 102, 125
  in East Home, 45, 50, 79, 112
  post-job correspondence with, 153, 154
  tricks on, 112, 119
Richardson, Dean, 224
Richardson, Mrs., 24, 47, 92
Richter, Bev, 121
Rinehart, Mrs., 24, 47, 92
Roberts, Gordon, 223
Roberts, Mary, 125

Robinson, Dr., 49, 65
Robinson, Sheila, 125
Rockefeller, Nelson, 188
Roe, Mrs., 19, 25
Romney, Gov. George, 188
Rothwell, Bob, 173
Rothwell, Floyd, 30, 132, **151,** 171
  bosses of, 85, 137
  construction input and, 67, 71, 100
  invitations from, 18, 51
  learning from, 59, 63, 64, 71
  meetings with, 25–26, 81, 202
  re-establishing friendship with, 165–166, 173
  working for, 55–59, 61, 66, 76, 82–83, 108, 114, 123, 160

S

Safety classes, 171, 200
Safety-pin strings, 69
Sanford, Virgil, 158
Sardone, Frank, **195,** 227, 230
  BHG president and CEO, 228-229, 239
  chats with, 163, 232
Sayre, Murray, 133, 167
Schau, Priscilla, 236
Schensul's Cafeteria, 95
Schmidt, Don, **192**
Scholten, Dr. Roger, medical center offices, 91
Schools of nursing. *See* Bronson Methodist Hospital School of Nursing; *and under* Western Michigan University, Bronson School of Nursing
Schott, Nancy, 121, **152**
Schrier, Dr. Paul, medical center offices, 91
Schultz, Roger, 223
Schwem, Jack, 177
Second Reformed Church, Kalamazoo, 223
Shafer, Ona, 107
Sheldon, Clark ("Mutt"), 114, 116, 153, 158
Sherwin–Williams paint store, 31
Sigma Gamma Hospital, Mount Clemens, 78, 94
Simmons, Mrs., 148
Slates, Harold, 177–178, 181
Smith, Ellis, **152**
Smith, Linda, 118
Smith, Marion, 35
Smith, Ruby, 72, 102
  chats with, 51–52, 71
  as Wesley Hall housekeeper, 40, 62, 68

Smoke-free policy, 197
Snack Bar Club, 147, 166
Snowstorms, 106, 182, 186, 207, 239
Snyder, Caspert and Harold, 186–187
Social Security coverage, 6, 95
Softball games, 35, 107, 162
  Bronson teams, 132–133, 156, 158, 169, **192,** 215, 241
Sootsman, Bill, **192,** 197, 216, 220, 236
Sopjes, Henry, 204
South Home, 21, 24, 49, 163, 216
  Christmastime festivities, 45–46
  gab sessions in, 35, 37
  housemothers at, 40, 43–44, 46, 49, 117
  kitchen supplies for, 14, 16–17
  replaced by new dorm, 119–120, 124
Southwestern Michigan Hospital Association of Engineers, 205
Spartz, Ed, 226
Spitters, Bertha, 29
Spriggs, Ruth, 109
Springgate, Dr. Roland, 156, 224
Stanley, Glenn, 25, 26

Starkweather, Jo, 188
State Theatre, Kalamazoo, 79, 157
Steeby, Mr., 2
Stell, Mrs. Mabel, 57, 65, **150,** 187, **192**
  communication lapses and, 84–85, 100–101
  remarried as Meyle, 167–168, **193**
Stevens, Jim, 204, 215
Stevenson, Mrs., 84–85
Stewart, Ralph, **151,** 200, 202
  crew cohesiveness and, 56, 58, 60, 237
  last days of, 228
  working in pairs with, 61, 114
Stiner, Judy, 106
Stroebel, James K., 200
Student nurses. *See* Nurses
Student nurses, education and training. *See* Bronson Methodist Hospital School of Nursing; *and under* Western Michigan University, Bronson School of Nursing
Stuteville, Mrs., 58
Summer Home Park, 68
Sun porches, 23, 128, 201
Sunbathing locations, 23

267

Sweet, Miss Leone, 15, 19, 153–154
  as classroom teacher, 48, 60, 68, 73, 94
  post-job contacts with, 153–154
Synwolt, Mrs., 117–118, 154
Szabo Company, 167

T
Talent shows, 48, 118, 156
Tarnow, Louise, 93
Tarnow Dairy, 93, 97
Tarr, Ralph, 103, 118
Taylor, Chuck, 119
Television, 44–45, 96, 116, 170
Tennis, 35, 68, 120
Thanksgiving, 26–28, 61, 209
Thomas, Nancy, 124
Thompson, Bob, 223–224
Thrasher, Julie, 236
Tiger games. *See* Detroit Tigers (baseball)
Tillie (kitchen supervisor), 22
Time cards, 21
Titus, John, 182
Tornadoes, 211
Tower, Pinkster and Titus Associates, 182, 210
Trade union elections, 198

Traffic tickets, 116
Trenery, Rev. Robert, 117, 170
Tribe, Jack, 35, 80, **152**
  coffee with, 25, 105
  crew cohesiveness and, 59, 97, 105, 113–114
  illnesses, 105, 113, 114
  as wall-washer, 39, 66
Troyer, Dean, **192**
Truesdale, Mr. and Mrs. George, 123
Truesdale Hall, 198
  celebrations in, 127–128, 158, 209
  construction of, 124, 126, 230
  demolition of, 229, 237
  facilities, 116, 127, 130–131, 197, 226, 229
  fundraising for, 122–123
  house/residence directors, 129, 147, 165
  nearby buildings, 175, 216
Truman, Mrs., 49
Tuberculosis Sanitarium, Kalamazoo, 113
Tuck, Mary, 106
Tunnels, 127, 128, 159, 232

268

Index

U
Uniforms, 156
  condition of, 19, 48, 106, 186
  naval reserve, **149**
  nurse, 80, 103, **150, 151**
  traditions with, 21, 69, 120
  nurse aide, 80
U. S. Navy, 77, 98, **149**, 164
University of Minnesota, School of Public Health, 183–184
Upjohn Company, 188, 203
  employees of, 104, 184, 199
Upjohn Park, 53
  facilities, 1, 2–3, 26, 35, 68

V
Vacations, 62, 219, 224, 237
Van Haaften, Bill, 35, 59
Van Loo twins, 2
VanBoven, Miss Adriana, 78
VandeGiessen, Sue Murray, 93, 236
VandenBerg, Roy, 25, **151, 152**
  crew cohesiveness and, 60, 202

VandenBerg, Roy, *cont.*
  in Floyd's office, 56, 58, 173
  home movies of, 80–81
  service award and retirement, 176, 177
  working in pairs on holidays with, 61, 176
Vander Molen, Abraham, 1, **86**
Vander Molen, Andy, 65, **88**, 109, 234
  as employee, 209, 240
Vander Molen, Cheryl ("Cheri") Lynn, 115, **194,** 216, 217, 233, 240
Vander Molen, Craig Alan, 119, 138–146, **192, 194,** 217, 222, 233, 240
Vander Molen, Donna, 240
Vander Molen, Elsie, **88**, 109, 210
Vander Molen, Esther, **88**, 240
Vander Molen, Evelyn, **88,** 109
Vander Molen, Gertrude ("Gert"), **88**, 234
Vander Molen, Jayne, **194,** 217, 222, 233
Vander Molen, Jim, **88**, 109

269

Vander Molen, Richard ("Dick")
adolescence, 2–3, 34, **86**, **88**, **89**
childhood, 1–2, **86**
family, 1–2, 64, 96–97, 109, 216–217, 239
formal schooling, 47, 97, 183–184
illnesses and injuries, 31–33, 78, 147–148, 189–190, 219
military service, 77, 98, **149**
on-the-job schooling (see Rothwell, Floyd, learning from)
parents, 1, 16, **86**
pets, 1, **86**, 209
residences, 1, 68, **86**, 110, 123, 125
sensitivities, 37, 66, 68, 81, 120, 226
siblings, 1, 6, 19, **88**, 109
Vander Molen, Richard ("Dick"), antics, 31, 81, 108, 116
"Man overboard," 20, 30, 42
Mrs. Ellis, 83, 96
Mrs. Lyons, 118
Mrs. Stell, 100–101
Mrs. Wright, 42, 45, 47, 52
nurses' aides and, 68

Vander Molen, Richard ("Dick"), antics, *cont.*
nurses and, 30, 31–33, 34, 42–43, 72, 92, 96, 106, 113, 114, 124, 128, **152**
in the hospital, 133–134, 153, 159
Vander Molen, Richard ("Dick"), honors
BMH School of Nursing, **193**, 209, 217–218
Christmas formal, **191**
fellow-employee tributes, 215-216, 237
portrait, 234
service awards, 52, 164, 203, 211, 214
Vander Molen, Richard ("Dick"), nicknames
Dick, the Buffer, 15, 39, 117
Dick, the Stud, 81
Dickie Boy, 39, 105
Jeff (of "Mutt and Jeff"), 114, 153
Mr. Bronson, 216
Vander Molen, Richard ("Dick"), occupations, 1, 2
animal care, 3–10, 53
electrician, 51, 55–60, 69–71, 84–85, 105,

270

Vander Molen, Richard ("Dick"), occupations,
electrician *cont.*
106, 107, 119, 120–121, 123, 124, **150, 151, 152**
in Bronson hospital, 130, 136, 147, 153, 155–156, 160–161, 169–170, 172, 198
in staff housing, 132, 163–164, 172, 188
in Truesdale Hall, 129–130
extracurricular, 77, 176, 208
dad, 142, 143–146, 178
handyman, 23–24, 82, 176
homebuilder, 123, 125
lay ministry, 178–180, 221, 241
messenger boy, 35–36
news reporter, 101, 105, 114, 167–168
outings coordinator, 168–169

Vander Molen, Richard ("Dick"), occupations,
extracurricular, *cont*
Santa Claus, **150,** 202
taxi driver, 65–66, 72, 106, 121–122
team sports, 35, **192,** 208, 215
janitor, 8–9, 13–18, 19–24, 28–31, 33, 40–41, 50, 52–53, 69
maintenance management, 187–188, 211-212
pleasures, 204–205
promotions, 175–178, 181–182, 212
stresses, 201, 210, 226
wall-washer, 39, 66–67, 97
Vander Molen, Richard ("Dick"), retirement, 232
BMH School of Nursing alumni activities, 224–225, 229–230

271

Vander Molen, Richard ("Dick"), retirement, *cont*
.church activities before and during, 221–223
food events in, 220, 223, 226, 233, 234
friends in, 227–228, 229, 235237, 236, 241
as hospital visitor escort, **196,** 220, 224, 230
last week at Bronson, 215–217
vacation travel in, **193,** 219, 224
writing for publications, 220, 225

Vander Molen, Richard ("Dick") and Betty ("Boop"), 166, **194,** 211, 224
car trips for married, 154, 221
children, 114–115, 118, 119, 123, 136–147, 155, **194** (*see also* individual names of)
as church youth sponsors, 198, 221–222
friends, 66, 162, 163, 167, 187, **195,** 219–220

Vander Molen, Richard ("Dick") and Betty ("Boop"), *cont*
grandchildren, **194,** 232–233
honors received by, 135–136, **195,** 230, 236
meeting, dating, courting, 69, 75–77, 93, 97

parties given in home, 134, 138
volunteers in retirement, **196,** 220–223, 224–225, 226, 230–231, 236
wedding and wedding anniversaries, 106, 109–110, **151, 195,** 233

Vander Molen, Steven Richard, 146–147, 155, 178, **194,** 211, 217, 233, 240
Vandernoot, Julie, 220
VanDusen, Dennis, **152**
Veld, Tom, 223
Vending machines, 20, 197
Viel, Harold, 182
Von Ehren, Warren, 80, 94, 103

Index

W

Wade, Bishop Raymond J., 67
Walker, Susan, 236
Wall-washers, 25, 39, 66–67, 97
Walvoord, Mark, 223-224
Walwood Hall, Western Michigan College, 34
Wantz, Miss Marie, 57, 82, 127, 133, 161
  Mary B. and, 162, 167
  retired to Fremont, Michigan, 162, 166–167
War efforts
  Cadet nurses in, 21, 24
  Guild women and, 4
  Korean War, 98
  World War II
    civilians, 176
    ends, 26–28, 158
    servicemen, 24, 98, 209
    veterans, 34, 61
Warren, Ken, 47
Washington Junior Hi School, 47
Waste disposal services, 57, 73, 133–134
Watson, Russell, 197, 208
Weber, Mrs. Helen, 147
  nursing education and, 94, 161–162, 165, 166, 209
  retirement, 166, 208

Weddings, 99, 105
  student nurses', 47, 77, 129, 136–137
  Vander Molen, 102, 106, 109–110, **151**
Weddle, Mr. Floyd, 118, 132, 158, 163
Weiandt, Linda, 157
Welch, Robin, 236
Wesbury, Stuart A., Jr., 164–165, 177
Wesley Hall aka "the big dorm," 35, 37, **90,** 106
  bicycle parking at back entrance, 21, 26, 55
  education at, vs. KHCS, 19, 43
  freshmen in, 19, 21, 28–29, 33, 42, 120
  housemothers, 92, 112, 117–118
  move to new dorm from, 127–128
  sign-out book in, 34, 48, 118
Wesley Hall aka "the big dorm," facilities, 33
  demolition of, **196,** 232, 237–238, 240
  elevator, 13–15, 20, 30, 48, 114
  infirmaries, 31
  libraries as study halls, 20
  nurses' rooms, 14–15

Wesley Hall aka "the big dorm," facilities, *cont.*
  plans for new dorm, 118, 119–120, 122–123 (*see also* Truesdale Hall)
  post-dorm hospital use, 189, 199
  smoking room, 31, **89**
  sun porch, 23
  tours of, **196,** 216, 230
West Medical Center, 201, 240
Westberg, Ward, 99, 164, 168, 175
  coffee with Dick, 177, 198
  as maintenance management, 180, 184–185, 203
  Southwestern Michigan Hospital Association of Engineers, 205
Western Michigan College (1942–1956), 34, 48, 103
  courses taken at, 69, 71, 119
  dating guys from, 73–74, 75–76
  freshmen bused to, 34, 126
Western Michigan University (1957–), 215
  Bronson School of Nursing (1999–), 231
  employees from, 136–137, 156, 175–176, 239
  Student Center, 209
Weston, Ellen, 237
White Caps (sports teams), 208
White Caps (yearbook), 52, 135–136, 188
White Cross Guild, 48, 68
  facilities funded by, 98–99, 122
  Guild House, 4–6, 7, 56, 73, **87**
Whitehead, Veva Lou, 36
Wiessner, Dick, 223
Wiessner, Dick and Lona, **195,** 219–220, 224
Wiggins, Bill, 25
Wills, Mrs., 106, 128, 154
Wilson, Dr. Doyle, **150,** 166
Window-washers, 25, 82
Wise, Myrt, 112
Wolters, Miss Dena, 57, 82, 123, 127, 133
  Lyle Nottingham and, 174
  Mary B. and, 162, 167

Wolters, Miss Dena, *cont.*
  retired to Fremont, Michigan, 162, 166–167
Wolthuis, Jack and Flo, 236
Woods Lake, trips to, 72
Work permits, 5, 6, 21, 28, 134
Wotring, Mrs., 117, 154
Wright, Mrs. ("Granny"), 62, **90,** 92
  Dick's games with, 42, 45, 47, 52, 70–71
  relationships with, 40, 43, 51–52, 53, 77, 92, 154
  wariness of being caught by, 66–67, 68, 69–70, 84
Wylie, Jackie Clark, 166, **193,** 208, 217

Y

Yardmen, 57, 172
Yearbooks, 120, 218. *See also White Caps*

Z

Zion Lutheran Church, Kalamazoo, 119, 126, 212
Zwart, Gordon, 182

The Bronson I Knew

To order more copies of

The Bronson I Knew,
Gone But Not Forgotten
by Dick Vander Molen

Each copy is $24.95 with 40% discount for 10 or more copies

   # copies _____ x _____ = $ _____

Shipping and Handling:
   USA Book Rate $3.00 for first book,
      $1.00 for each additional book. $ _____

Tax: Michigan residents, add 6% sales tax $ _____

                        Total $ _____

Checks payable to:
Alumni Association of BMH School of Nursing

Mail order form and payment to:
   Alumni Association of BMH School of Nursing
   202 Brittany Dr.
   Portage, MI   49024

Send book/s to (please print):

Name_____

Street _____

City_____

State/Province_____Zip _____

Please allow three weeks for delivery.